DISCOVERING A LARGER GOD

Praise for *Discovering a Larger God*

Ambushed by Jesus, just as I was, born again in midlife, John Andrews has kept reaching back to help others find their way out of darkness as he did. He writes with the fervency of a convert and the urgency of a man on a mission.

LEE STROBEL
New York Times best-selling author

John Andrews chronicles his remarkable journey to faith in this beautiful collection of essays. He offers a poignant and challenging look at what it truly means to follow Christ as he meets the real, living God of Scripture.

KATHERINE BEIM-ESCHE
Executive Director, Fellowship of Former Christian Scientists

As a fourth-generation follower of the Christian Science religion, Andrews came to realize that it downplayed the presence of sin and evil, denied the reality of death, diminished the greatness of Jesus the Son of God, and devalued his saving work of atonement on the cross. Now in these pages we can follow him on his journey out of self-salvation and into the glorious freedom of the gospel.

DONALD SWEETING
President, Colorado Christian University
Former President, Reformed Theological Seminary

With well-structured arguments, personal transparency, and a love for his audience, John brings out the richness of biblical Christianity in contrast to the cruel spiritual poverty of Christian Science.

LINDA KRAMER
Author of *Perfect Peril: Christian Science and Mind Control*

Leaving the cult of Christian Science can be a daunting task, as John Andrews found. It means escaping an Alice-in-Wonderland world where nothing is as it seems. This is the story of John's long and painful struggle to reconcile the vast deception of a dangerous counterfeit with the truth of the Bible. With reasoned logic and probing questions, he provides the reader a roadmap to real health and true intimacy with the God of all creation.

ROBERT PARDON
Director, New England Institute of Religious Research

Discovering a Larger God speaks convincingly that Christian Scientists can't save themselves through studying *Science and Health*, nor should they. Through articulate and convincing essays, John Andrews weaves biblical truth into the heart of the reader assuring them that peace can be found if only they relinquish control to the Savior himself.

LAUREN HUNTER
Author of *Leaving Christian Science: 10 Stories of New Faith in Jesus Christ*

John Andrews gives us the fruit of a keen mind and grace-soaked heart which will serve any seeker who feels a curious stirring about the nature and personhood of God. Here is a clear-thinking examination not only of Christian Science but of the many offerings of self-salvation in the buffet of modern spirituality. Sit with my friend as he shares with you the treasures found when he "discovered a larger God in the Crucified One."

DOUG BROWN
Lead Pastor, Greenwood Community Church, Denver, Colorado

Also by John Andrews

Mort: A Memoir
(2020)

Downstream: An American Album
(With Jim Andrews, 2018)

Backbone Colorado USA: Dispatches from the Divide
(2015)

Responsibility Reborn: A Citizen's Guide to the Next American Century
(2011)

The Andrews of Principia: 100 Years of an American Family
(Editor, 1996)

With You Always: Jesus in the Hymns of Mary Baker Eddy
(1988)

Life Lessons of a Former Christian Scientist

DISCOVERING A LARGER GOD

How the Cross Prevails Where Self-Salvation Fails

John Andrews

For
CARL GANS
(1949–2011)

*"Run with patience the race that is set before us,
looking unto Jesus, the author and finisher
of our faith" (Hebrews 12:1, 2).*

WHY THIS BOOK?

"This isn't working. I've been misled, harmed, ill served. I want out. I need to find a better way of life." So may run the thoughts of someone feeling trapped in an unhealthy belief system or sub-culture. The need to escape can become overwhelming.

For me in midlife, what I had to escape was Mary Baker Eddy's system known as Christian Science. I felt its untruths about God and man pushing me out, even as the Bible's truths about the God-man, Jesus Christ, were pulling me out.

After finally breaking free in the 1990s, I undertook an online ministry in the spirit of "Come, let us reason together" (Isaiah 1:18) for others who were questioning Christian Science or had left. My writings from two decades of that work are collected here.

The ministry is named for Ananias, who baptized Saul of Tarsus. Like them, I discovered a larger God in the Crucified One. Do you know Him?

*Not a cold divine Principle, but a Father who comes running.
See the final essay in Chapter 7 (Luke 15:20).*

TABLE OF CONTENTS

PROLOGUE: MY DISCOVERY I

CHAPTER 1: WHAT IS MAN, THAT THOU ART MINDFUL OF HIM?..1

    Facing Up to Who I Was..3

CHAPTER 2: WHAT SHALL I DO WITH JESUS WHO IS CALLED CHRIST?..25

    I Thought I Was a Christian 27
    What Two of Us Decided to Do 29
    Once Blind, Now Seeing 34
    To Know Only Christ Crucified...35
    Ready to Enthrone Him? 37

CHAPTER 3: WHAT IF THE BIBLE IS ITS OWN KEY? 41

    Locked Out No More 43
    To Have the Mind of Christ 44
    To Keep Faith With Paul..46
    To Act with the Apostles 47
    Combating the Enemy 49
    Contesting for Truth..52
    Finding the True Bread...56

CHAPTER 4: A GLORIOUS CHURCH, HOLY AND PERFECT?.........59

    No Jesus, No Church..61
    What They're Missing...62
    My Morning Meal..64

Hymns for Him 67
Broken Cisterns 69
Not Reinvented 71
Sunset for Eddyism...77

CHAPTER 5: WHY TAKE HER WORD FOR IT?...............**83**

Someone to Revere?..85
Full of Herself...89
Revising the Trinity 92
Therapeutics or Salvation? 93
Mbe's Pride or Job's Humility?...99
No Natal Hour 103
Sisterhood Ascendant..106
Isn't It Tragic...108

CHAPTER 6: ARE YOU REALLY SEEKING TRUTH? **113**

Impossible Straddle...115
Family Isn't God 118
Best Day of My Life...121
Designer Spirituality Defrauds 123
Thinking Makes It So?..127
Tyranny of the Insecure 128
A Grandson's Prayer 130
Talking Past Each Other...132
Down the Generations 134
The Narrow Gate 136

CHAPTER 7: COULD WE TRY TALKING IT OVER? **141**

The Dare..143
Wes Backs Away..145
Jack Takes the Plunge...150
Diminishing Jesus..153
Much to Atone for..155
Why Settle for Less? 157
Weigh the Evidence..158
Pathways for Dialogue..160
Shopping for a Home 166
A Father Who Comes Running..177

CHAPTER 8: WHAT BETTER PLACE TO TAKE MY STAND? 181
Not by Chance 183
My Doorway Out..185
Undone 187
Born to Adore..188
In Plain Sight 191

CHAPTER 9: HOW CAN I EVER THANK HIM ENOUGH? 195
Celebrating Our Rebirth 197
Adoration Unreserved 206
An Old Psalm Read Anew 211
Rescued to Be Rescuers..214

EPILOGUE: SEVEN WINDOWS ON A LIFE 221
A Self-Interview 223

CONCLUSION OF THE MATTER...231

**APPENDIX A: THE HOUND OF HEAVEN BY FRANCIS
THOMPSON**..233

APPENDIX B: THE APOSTLES' CREED 239

INDEX: CITATIONS FROM THE BIBLE & MARY BAKER EDDY ..241

ACKNOWLEDGMENTS...247

ABOUT THE AUTHOR 249

"Ananias putting his hands on him said, Brother Saul, the Lord, even Jesus, hath sent me, that thou mightest receive thy sight" (Acts 9:17).

PROLOGUE:
My Discovery

What's a man to do when he discovers there is far more to this thing called "God" than he was led to believe all his life? What I felt compelled to do was to risk everything and follow hard after that newly encountered God, no matter the cost.

Taken by Storm

I was raised in the Christian Science religion as founded by Mary Baker Eddy about 1870 and as followed by four generations in my family since about 1900.

She called her system a new discovery about what is real and true, who God is. This book is about my counter-discovery of old verities that have proved more life-giving and reliable than all her innovations.

I had indeed found what was, to me, an admirable God in the teachings of Mrs. Eddy in the first forty years of my life. But then I found a truly awesome God, the Adorable One, in the pages of the Bible. This God soon took me by storm.

Had to Follow

This was a larger God, a God who was willing and able to do amazing things that Mrs. Eddy's God could not or would not do. I just had to follow this wonderful God. I just had to give myself to him totally.

This God could and did make the whole world around us, the actual physical universe. That God whom Mrs. Eddy presented did not make any of it.

This God could and did create the human me, all of me, body and mind, heart and soul, the person that I am here and now, and all the human beings that people my world. That God, again, did nothing of the kind.

This God, in designing me as an improbable blend of matter and spirit, accorded me the dignity of freely choosing to accept or reject his authority over my life—and the responsibility of living forever with the consequences of my choice. That God gave me no such freedom.

Impossible, She Said

This God could and did clothe himself in human form to live among men for a few years as Jesus Christ, and to die at the hands of men in proof of his infinite forgiveness for the sin that corrupts me and everyone else.

Whereas being made flesh as a helpless baby, tramping the dusty roads of Palestine as an itinerant preacher, or bleeding on the cross as a lamb of sacrifice, are all deemed impossible for that God whom Mrs. Eddy presents.

This God who exists as one supreme being in three persons, Father, Son, and Holy Spirit, can literally indwell my physical and mental being with the Holy Spirit.

This God, again through the Holy Spirit, can knit together my being with that of other believers so that all of us are joined as one indivisible Body of Christ, no less tangibly than Jesus' own fingers were joined to his hands when he lived here among us.

That God whose synonyms I learned in Christian Science was not a spirit capable of involving itself that way with human beings individually or collectively.

As for Me

When the Scriptures invited me to follow a larger, closer, kinder God, a God who is truly omnipotent and Lord of all, in contrast to the deity of limits and boundaries presented by Mrs. Eddy, what could I do but obey?

Others may, for reasons of taste or loyalty, prefer that smaller God regardless. But some of us will feel compelled to say with Joshua, "As for me and my house, we will serve the Lord" (Joshua 24:15).

This prologue, up to here, was written in 1998; what follows, I've added in 2020. Ninety-eight was five years after I became a baptized Christian, 18 years after I gave my life to Jesus Christ, and 39 years after I first joined the Christian Science Church. I was then 54.

Soon afterward, working with the late Carl Gans, I started the Ananias website. Named for the hesitant but obedient disciple at Damascus who participated in St. Paul's conversion (Acts 9:10), the site has served since 2000 as an outreach to others who might be questioning Christian Science.

An Invitation to Converse

Some fifty essays I wrote for Ananias.org over the years comprise the book in your hands. The collection is organized around nine big questions a current or former Scientist needs to grapple with. It's presented not as a structured argument but as an open conversation. You'll find it, as such, readily accessible, I believe. Begin anywhere and make your own way.

The book invites a diverse readership. You may know little about Mary Baker Eddy's religion, or a great deal. If the latter, you may have never embraced it, have ceased embracing it, or may still embrace it. Whichever of those happens to be the case, I hope this can be for you and me an amicable venture in mutual understanding, a source not of heat but of light.

I offer it to the glory of Him who lived, died, rose, and reigns as light and life for us all, the Good Shepherd who lovingly rescued me from the dead end of self-salvation, Jesus the Carpenter of Nazareth.

Expulsion of Adam and Eve from Paradise (Dore)

CHAPTER 1:
WHAT IS MAN, THAT THOU ART MINDFUL OF HIM?[1]

God's perfect child, spiritual not material, sinless, no relation to Adam? The metaphysical "me" I heard about from church services and *Science and Health* didn't match the all-too-human me I saw in the mirror. My "inward man" was more and more a perishing sinner as self-love had its way.[2] A reckoning awaited. Jesus had a due bill for me—and a rescue plan.

[1] Psalm 8:4

[2] II Corinthians 4:16

FACING UP TO WHO I WAS

He Followed Me

I wasn't always a follower of Jesus Christ. For a long time I was into self-salvation. It took until I was almost forty for the Hound of Heaven, as a poet has called him, to pursue and woo and finally win me. You might say Jesus followed me before I followed him.

But no one was ever more joyously born again. No haughty heart was ever more abjectly humbled. It was the defining event of an eventful life. I'm writing about it here at length for the first time because, as the old hymn says, "I love to tell the story" — and because of what my experience can teach us about the big lie of self-salvation.

For self-salvation takes many subtle forms in these hubristic times of ours. As old as the Tower of Babel, as new as the Freedom Tower, it's really most people's mode of coping. The Religion of Me is all around us, much of the time in attractive non-religious guise.

But whether packaged as lifestyle, politics, faith, or some hip hybrid, this individualistic mass cult can't fulfill its promises. I learned the hard way that self-salvation is ultimately a fraud and a failure.

Deceptive Veneer

Early on, though, things were great. My boyhood and early adulthood had been a happy and rewarding time. Friends knew me as a spiritually engaged, morally serious, materially successful young guy. I was active in church and devoted to my wife and our three children. I loved my life and everything about it.

Not really knowing Jesus, I still revered God, lived by prayer, and studied the Bible every day. That's because four generations of my family and three generations of Donna's had been faithful churchgoers in the tradition of Mary Baker Eddy, a self-taught prophetess who left Congregationalism in 1875 to found her own new church, Christian Science.

The tenets of Christian Science as presented in Eddy's text-book, *Science and Health with Key to the Scriptures*, have a deceptive veneer of similarity to what true Christians believe. They deny key elements of the gospel, however.

Despite professing that "we take the inspired word of the Bible as our sufficient guide to eternal life…we acknowledge God's forgiveness of sin…[and] we acknowledge Jesus' atonement" (SH 497), Christian Scientists redefine or qualify those familiar concepts to the point of meaninglessness.

Eddy twists Scripture to ostensibly prove her depiction of God as impersonal and unitarian ("divine Principle") and of humanity as sinless but deceived (asleep in an "Adam dream"). She claims to have discerned rules and examples in the Bible by which the individual can wake himself from dreaming and begin exercising the dominion granted mankind in Genesis 1.

By deeming Christ's statement, "I and my Father are one" (John 10:30), applicable to anyone thus awakened, she demotes Jesus from God the Son to something like our peer, "the highest human concept of the perfect man" (SH 482:19).

The resulting belief system is a heady mixture of ancient Gnosticism, liberal Protestantism, the higher criticism, and New England transcendentalism with its fashionable Eastern mystic tinges. Today's prosperity gospel, designer spirituality, and New Age self-help movements are foreshadowed even in the pre-1900 beginnings of Christian Science.

No Sin, No Savior

I have to stress, though, how earnestly (if shallowly) biblical and conventionally American our way of life was when I was growing up in the Eisenhower years. Our family was steeped in Scripture, regular at church on Sundays and Wednesdays, faithful with the Lord's Prayer, abstinent from drugs and alcohol, spiritually devout in every way.

We thought Christian Science was just another religious denomination, though more correct because we met health needs by prayer, not medicine, and more Christlike because we had the supposed key to the Scriptures with its "final revelation" of God and man and truth (SH 107:5).

What that so-called revelation told us, told me, was that by knowing this truth I could think my way to health, happiness, and holiness in this world, and guarantee myself heaven in the next. In other words, self-salvation. They didn't call it that, but that's what it amounted to.

Christian Science, despite its occasional odd references to Jesus as the Savior, assured me I was in no way a sinner in need of a savior. And it waved off the superstitious notion that our Lord's death on the cross had redeemed me or anybody from a lost condition. All that was "old theology."

So was Jesus God incarnate? Certainly not, we were taught. Nor did Jesus even really die. His death was but a "seeming." Nor was that atonement mentioned in our tenets an actual substitutionary sacrifice. It was merely a "demonstration," a sort of how-to lesson for our benefit, carried out by a "Way-shower" (SH 497:15).

Self-Salvation

As strange as this belief system might seem, viewed with a secular perspective from outside; as obvious a spiritual counterfeit as it might be to the well-taught Christian, it felt like a satisfying and rewarding way of life most of the time to those of us living it from the inside.

Maturing into marriage and military service soon after college, I happily went with the flow of a religious subculture imbued in me by having gone to school with fellow Christian

Scientists in Missouri and Illinois for 16 years and to summer camp with them in Colorado for 12 years.

I taught Sunday school, took on church leadership duties, received class instruction, wrote for the church periodicals, and joined the staff of Adventure Unlimited, the Christian Science youth ministry my parents had founded. I was all in for Christian Science; all in for self-salvation.

What I didn't realize, during those years of my twenties and thirties, was how patiently and purposefully Christ was pursuing me all the while. My heart was haughty indeed; not with harsh arrogance, perhaps, but with a quiet, complacent sort of spiritual superiority and smugness, rooted in the Mary Baker Eddy assurance that with sufficient mental discipline I would always be captain of my own destiny. No flicker of doubt or inadequacy disturbed that certitude.

So sure of who God was and was not, I didn't hear behind me what Francis Thompson, in his long impassioned poem about the Hound of Heaven, calls "those strong feet that followed, followed after with unhurrying chase, deliberate speed, majestic instancy."[3] It was always there, the relentless tread of God the Son, Jesus our elder brother, implacable in his loving design to corner me and rescue me — but I was deaf to it.

Chain Links

The Lord providentially used people and experiences and books, inward longings and outward circumstances and little moments, to weave a net of necessity and logic around me that gradually drew closed until I was broken and taken.

My conversion needed many links in the chain, many blows of the ax. I emphasize this to encourage believers in the small acts of witnessing that may become links in the conversion chain for

---

[3] See poem in Appendix A, first stanza

someone else — someone whose new birth we ourselves may never see, but whose soul God will never abandon.

So as I look back now, there are all these snapshots in my treasured album. An encounter with someone, a sentence from a book, a verse in Scripture that nagged at me, an hour alone when ugly self-knowledge became unavoidable, burn in my memory down the years. Each was a waypoint along the winding path of a lost sheep's dumb refusal to face and follow the Savior, and his gracious refusal to stop following me. Here are a few of my snapshots:

The Cadet

One evening at naval officer school, I'm confronted by a fellow cadet who asks if I have any idea how blatantly the Christian Science textbook, open on my desk, falsifies the Gospel. I am lost and will remain so, he tells me, until I place the crucified and risen Lord Jesus at the center of my life.

It was, I saw later, rather like the scene in Acts 8 where Philip asks the queen's treasurer if he understands the messianic prophecy in Isaiah. But unlike that teachable Ethiopian, I was nowhere near ready to be evangelized, let alone baptized.

Our exchange, two or three uncomfortable minutes at most, ended inconclusively. I never forgot it, though. I never will.

The Convert

Years pass. One morning in Washington, I'm present at a small prayer breakfast in the White House staff mess where Nixon hatchet man Chuck Colson, facing indictment by the Watergate prosecutors, movingly recounts his conversion from lapsed Catholic to born-again evangelical Christian.

Colson in tears? Could it be? I meet with him later to learn more of the story. It's Jesus, he tells me. "I needed him and so do you. Get to know Jesus, John."

Chuck sends me home with a copy of *Mere Christianity* by C. S. Lewis, a book and an author I had never heard of before. But I didn't read a word of it, not then and not for a long time after. I kept it, though. I always will.

The Youth Worker

The scene shifts to Colorado. Leading the Adventure Unlimited youth organization, I struggle with how to get teenagers interested in the abstruse, abstract teachings of Christian Science.

Brushes with winsome evangelical leaders such as Jim Groen of Youth for Christ, Denny Rydberg of Youth Specialties, and Don Reeverts of Young Life start me thinking that one thing our programs need is more of Jesus. But my tentative efforts in that direction meet resistance. I back off and try another angle, taking a friend's dare to write a lesson plan on 100 ways our volunteers could engage kids with the Bible. "Chart of Life," it was called, echoing an Eddy phrase (SH 24:8). More resistance.

Vexed and perplexed, I find myself wondering who these people are anyway, these Christian Scientists. This church I grew up in and am now trying to serve, ostensibly part of the Body of Christ; really?

The Authors

Next begins the attack of the authors. I'm gripped with a strange new hunger for wider and deeper views of God. *Mere Christianity* comes off my shelf, onto my desk, and is devoured. Why wasn't I told about this sooner?

Then more of C. S. Lewis, then George MacDonald, John Henry Newman, G. K. Chesterton, Malcolm Muggeridge, Josh McDowell. Then J. B. Phillips' *Your God is Too Small*. The more I read, the more I have to read. Why have the Trinity and Jesus in his fullness been kept from me for so long?

Then I attend a week of lectures by Carl F. H. Henry at Denver Seminary; an odd place for the local Christian Science first reader to turn up. The eminent theologian's quiet intensity arrests me. There is something humbly holy about him; disturbing yet irresistible.

We must know Jesus in the exact way Scripture presents him, or not know him at all, Henry insists in one talk. The earnest young student of Mrs. Eddy's Christological revisionism goes home unsettled.

But New Age tempters are hounding my other flank. Free-thinking Christian Science friends introduce me to the likes of Teilhard de Chardin, Barbara Marx Hubbard, and the *Course on Miracles*. Tasting their racy allure, at once magnetic and repellent, I begin to see the easy corruptibility of Eddy's self-invented spirituality. Have I built my life on rock or sand?

The Serpent

Things are coming to a head. About this time, the serpent finds another entry into my ill-defended citadel: the lust of the flesh. A foolish infatuation at the office crosses the line into marital infidelity.

She and I both "knew better," but neither of us recoiled much from "sinning against God." Those scare quotes suggest the bland detachment that the two of us as Scientists granted ourselves from the ugly reality of sin.

Found out, ashamed, facing divorce, devastated but not really broken, I am unable to identify any longer as God's perfect child, untainted by matter and evil. Looking within, I see only dark depravity. I have failed my wife and kids, and self-salvation has failed me.

The Sisters

That's where matters stood in July 1980, the summer of my 37th year. "Nought shelters thee who wilt not shelter Me," Thompson's Hound of Heaven warns the fugitive soul.[4] I was reaching that point without fully realizing it. Christian Science was losing its

---

[4] See poem in Appendix A, 3rd stanza

power to meet my needs or explain my world, let alone wash me clean.

"Lost indeed, escape is none," cries another of the old devotional poets, George MacDonald, when the Good Shepherd's dogs finally corner him. Just so: confident John had run out of options, and one ringing telephone was soon to prove it.

"Line 1 is for you," the receptionist at our Adventure Unlimited headquarters office told me. "It's Carol Wilson in Pasadena. Her daughter is at camp right now." But the distraught mother wasn't calling about Annie, 16, then attending the A/U Ranches in Buena Vista, Colorado, with hundreds of other Christian Science teens. It was her older daughter, Laurie, 19, that Mrs. Wilson urgently hoped I could help.

Laurie, she explained, had been to our camp in past years, but was spending this summer in Boulder with a group of fellow Stanford students, doing street evangelism for InterVarsity Christian Fellowship. The girl had gone off to college last fall as a devoted young Christian Scientist, Carol told me, but then "the fundamentalists captured her."

Would I, as a favor to the worried family, make contact with Laurie and take her to visit Annie at camp, thus hopefully "waking her up" to return to the Christian Science fold? Doubtful as the errand seemed, the mother's anguish touched me. I agreed to try.

To Boulder

Mark Reed, the young Presbyterian pastor leading the InterVarsity group in Boulder, was friendly and relaxed when I reached him by phone and outlined the situation. Could we meet and explore options? Sure, he said; come Thursday about 5:30. (Mark, Carol, Annie, and Laurie are pen names used here to protect those individuals' privacy.)

I assured him my approach would be respectful of Laurie Wilson's autonomy as a young adult, "and by the way, I happen to be a Christian Scientist who considers himself a Christian first and foremost." Mark voiced polite skepticism at this, having roomed with a Christian Scientist in college. "You'll see," I promised. But the one who was destined to see was me.

Spaghetti and salad were being served on paper plates to Mark's gang when I found my way into the big rented house near the University of Colorado campus. Laurie seemed sweet, serious, a little shy. Mark was just as he had been on the phone, engaging and talkative, never met a stranger. The kids were quick to make me welcome, though I could sense their curiosity about this guy from a church many regarded as a cult.

But I hadn't been there five minutes when a feeling I had never experienced before shot through me like high voltage — as tangibly as if I'd put my finger in a light socket. Joining hands in a circle, they prayed aloud for Jesus to be present at this meal and all evening, and at that moment I knew him to be real and near in a whole new way. "Whatever it is you people have," I heard myself thinking, "I need it and I want it."

As dusk came on, Mark divided everyone into teams and we fanned out along the Pearl Street mall to strike up conversations with whoever might be willing. Nothing sticks with me from what was said that night — or the next night either, for they prevailed on me to come back, all unplanned.

But there was a mounting sense of destiny, tectonic plates inexorably shifting, as my complacent certainty that I understood the Bible much better than they did, gave way inch by inch and hour by hour in our moonlight discussions on the grass beside the mall.

To Camp

After two evenings together, it was agreed. Laurie and Mark would come with me the following Tuesday for a day trip to visit Annie at the A/U camp. More hours together on the road; more theological jousting; and again, there was no decisive exchange I could point to, but simply that ever-greater longing to come in from the cold and have the kind of personal relationship with Jesus Christ, Savior and Lord, that these new friends of mine had.

Round-Up Ranch campers were thronging in to lunch when we arrived. The sisters hugged, giggled, and chattered as girls will do. It was clear to me there was to be no going back by Laurie from her newfound faith, nor by then did I want her to. God's target all along in this rescue operation had been John, the ostensible rescuer, I was starting to see. And right there in the dining hall, the net closed around me at last.

Camp activities on Tuesday afternoon always paused for a youth-led testimonial meeting (similar to the Wednesday evening service in Christian Science churches) at which teens would tell what God was doing in their lives. Sitting near the back with Reed and the Wilson girls, I squirmed uncomfortably as the reader presented Bible selections out of context and *Science and Health* passages of blurry metaphysics, followed by several campers' simple accounts of how "knowing the truth" had helped them.

Afterward, when Annie had said her goodbyes and the lodge had emptied out, I felt too awful for words. My Christian Science kids had shown so poorly. This wasn't really them at their best, I stammered to my friends. Mark must have sensed I was at a tipping point. His gentleness right then will stay with me as long as I live.

Finally Ready

"Don't be hard on yourself, John, or hard on them. Listening to them, I can tell they are good kids. Great kids. But what's missing when they talk, don't you think, is Jesus. You just need to help them put Jesus at the center."

Right there at the Colorado camp, my family's own camp, where so much of my spiritual formation had happened since boyhood, Mark Reed was making the very same appeal that Chuck Colson had made to me in a Washington law office seven years before — "Get to know Jesus; you need him" — but now I was finally ready to listen.

And more than listen; I was ready to submit. After Mark said that, the dam of my emotions broke, and with it my will to resist. I just put my head in my hands and sobbed.

They didn't lead me through the sinner's prayer, nor did I physically kneel. The place was too public. But then and there I did ask Jesus to be on the throne of my heart. I accepted him as Lord of my life. I prostrated myself spiritually to the God-man, and my world has never been the same from that moment on.

Unheard Of

Wednesday: the first day of the rest of my life. The Hound of Heaven had run to ground my haughty heart. In the poem, Thompson speaks of being driven to his knees and left "defenseless, utterly," by the severity of God's all-demanding love. [5] That's where this born-again Christian Scientist woke to find himself.

My shattered self-sufficiency echoed the brokenness of the Psalmist: "So foolish was I, and ignorant; I was as a beast before thee" (Ps. 73:22). Jesus hounds us down, though, only to lift us up. I at once saw his pierced hand "outstretched caressingly," as Thompson puts it, and heard his invitation: "Rise, clasp my hand, and come." [6]

My next chapter, soon to slow like a glacier, unfolded initially at lightspeed.

Rashly, but unable to do otherwise, that very Wednesday evening I challenged our Christian Science congregation at the close of the testimonial meeting to do better in rendering Jesus the "endless homage" that Mary Baker Eddy says we owe him (SH 18:5).

My outburst from the first reader's desk had violated a taboo, and there was a storm. Despite Eddy's assertion on the first page

---

[5] See poem in Appendix A, 7th stanza

[6] See poem in Appendix A, last stanza

of her textbook that "the time for thinkers has come," doctrinal disputation and correction among Scientists outside the Boston hierarchy is unheard of.

By Thursday evening, my resignation as reader had been demanded by the local members. I willingly gave it — feeling, by then, no more in command of events than a leaf in a hurricane. The congregation needed someone more docile in that role, and I needed some time away to make sense of the past week's spiritual upheaval.

Long Goodbye

So was I finished with Christian Science? Not yet; not nearly. The Hound of Heaven still had years of hard lessons to teach me, before I would come to the point of renouncing the Eddy fallacy entirely.

But my fateful encounter with the Wilson family and Mark Reed during that week in July had brought the breakthrough. After a lifetime of denying I was a sinner in need of a savior, I had bowed to own myself exactly that. From the haughtiness of rejecting what the Apostles' Creed proclaims about Christ and his Cross, God and his Church, I had meekly embraced it all. Or much of it, anyway.

However, because something in our human makeup wants to say with Paul, "so worship I the God of my fathers" (Acts 24:14), and because my whole way of life was woven in with Christian Scientists and the Christian Science movement, disengaging from all that took time.

Thus Donna and I and our children continued attending Sixth Church, ignoring fellow members' unspoken questions about my weird new views. I continued seeking to teach Sunday school and publish in the periodicals, meeting a wall of unexplained rejection that I later learned was purposeful. John Andrews Jr. was black-listed.

I did leave my job at Adventure Unlimited within a few months, too torn about the claims of Science to go on advocating them to young people. Yet I found myself studying *Science and*

Health more avidly than ever, determined to somehow reconcile it with the biblical truth I now placed uppermost. I even ventured into the tall weeds with maverick Scientists working to validate prayer-treatment through lab experiments.

And all the while I read more and more of everything I could find by G. K. Chesterton, George MacDonald, and C. S. Lewis. My conversion in its fullness occurred, I guess you'd say, with a slow-motion pace similar to Lewis's own, as narrated in his autobiography, *Surprised by Joy*.

Tower of Pride

The road I walked during that decade of the 1980s, often in spite of myself, is well described in Lewis's mordant observation from Chapter XIV of that book:

> Really, a young Atheist cannot guard his faith too
> carefully. Dangers lie in wait for him on every side.
> You must not do, you must not even try to do, the
> will of the Father unless you are prepared to "know
> of the doctrine."

Not from atheism as such, but from a self-made tower of intellectual and spiritual pride that was no less God-defying in its own way, I had thought to approach the Father on my terms, not his, retaining ultimate control. It was impossible.

Yet even after taking its decisive fall in the lodge at camp, that foolish project kept hold of me much longer than I like to admit. Looking back, I can see that my situation in those years was like Thompson's description of himself in "The Hound of Heaven":

> For though I knew His love who followed,
> Yet was I sore adread, lest having Him,

I should have nought beside.[7]

My fallback position, after haughtily resisting the Lord Jesus for so long and at last (conditionally) yielding, was to bargain for terms with him in hope of hanging on to at least some part of the old familiar Eddy beliefs. Only very gradually did it become clear that he would not take less than all of me.

What Jesus says about one's inescapably coming to "know of the doctrine" about the Son—the Trinity, the Incarnation, the Atonement—as a result of trying to obey the Father (quoted above by Lewis from John 7:17) came gloriously true for me.

The more I embraced that doctrine, the less I was able to stomach Eddy's contrary metaphysics when reading her book or attending services. Cautiously seeking the ear of fellow Scientists, I was everywhere ignored or rebuffed. Restlessly sampling the worship experience at churches of other denominations, I was on some Sundays a hungry man finding bread, on others merely an idler, a spiritual tourist.

The sharp turn in my faith left Donna wondering who her husband was now anyway, and I couldn't blame her. And just when our marriage seemed reborn, my weakness triggered another crisis and forced us to start over yet again. It was a strange, uncertain time for our whole family.

Vertical & Horizontal

But I sensed a bigger picture coming into focus as my work in public policy engaged me more deeply with the foundations of a free society and the sources of collectivism. I began to see how the self-salvation temptation in human affairs is all of one piece.

Whether we are participating in religious life or political governance, making a living with our work or making a life with

[7] See poem in Appendix A, first stanza

our families and communities, the false confidence that "I've got this" or "we can do it" keeps obscuring our radical need for God's truth and love, God's presence and power. We cannot, in fact, "do it." Not by ourselves, not humanly, for the things that matter most.

The same utopian illusion of human perfectibility in an imperfect world that anciently lured Adam and Eve to eat of the forbidden tree, and later enticed the builders of Babel to erect a tower to heaven, operates today in the hubris of progressive politics and scientism, the seductions of hard and soft Marxism, and the subjectivity of liberal theology in its many guises, Christian Science included.

Self-salvation is always a cheat. Always. The horizontal possibilities of mankind's innovation and cooperation, vast and marvelous as they are, face not only the frustration of failure but ultimately the doom of disaster unless they are supernaturally steadied and secured by the vertical authority of a sovereign and saving God.

Horizontal and vertical, intersecting and interacting: the coordinates of the Cross confront us here, and it's no accident. They are inescapable. Christian Science or Eddyism or self-salvation held less and less sway over me with the dawning of these realizations.

Marks of a Gnostic

My driven sense of mission to tell Scientists about Jesus was the last thing to yield. Subtly the impulse of being a savior to others had replaced the notion of saving myself. I was still stuck on the horizontal plane, and dogged about it.

There had to be a way. I wrote a little book about how the Savior's person and teachings permeate Mary Baker Eddy's seven poems at the center of the Christian Science hymnal.[8] I created the

---

[8] *With You Always: The Presence of Jesus in Mary Baker Eddy's Hymns* can be ordered from the Ananias.org home page.

fictional Tim Ryan, a young rebel with one foot in the Christian Science healing practice and the other in Catholic spirituality, and spun a series of short stories about him. All in vain.

How repulsive, one day after long years of this, to recognize in myself all the marks of a Pharisee or a Gnostic — less a beneficiary of grace than a violator of it. So proud was I of knowing what they didn't; so scornful of them for not seeing in the Bible what was plain to me on every page.

The ugliness brought me up short. I had become the very hypocrite that Christ died to save me from being. That did it. No more ingesting poison. This needed to stop.

I needed to cut cleanly and get out. One November day in 1992, a full dozen years after the July day at camp, I at last resigned my membership in the Christian Science mother church and our local branch.

Homecoming

One April night in 1993, now worshipping with a small Anglican congregation near my home, where the rector, Father John Andrews (God's sense of humor is so divine), explained I couldn't have communion until baptized, I tearfully received baptism and formally joined the Body of Christ, aged 49 years.

So ends this fugitive's story of what Francis Thompson calls "that long pursuit" by the Hound of Heaven.[9] It was for me exactly as he tells it in the poem's closing lines, a tender homecoming to the Savior's arms and a declaration in the Lord's own words as direct as what he gave the man born blind, the woman at the well, or Moses at the bush: "I am He whom thou seekest."[10]

Nothing can express my abounding joy, then and ever since then, at having been pursued, turned, taken, and made new as I

[9] See poem in Appendix A, 9th stanza

[10] See poem in Appendix A, last stanza

was by our implacably gracious Redeemer. "Thanks be to God for his unspeakable gift" (II Cor. 9:15).

Now in closing, let me address a couple of final questions: What's the rest of the story, three decades on? And what are the takeaways, the lessons from all this?

Further Up

The adventure of following Jesus never really ends or even pauses. To that extent, my father and mother were indeed divinely guided in naming their youth ministry for Christian Scientists, Adventure Unlimited. More's the pity that they scarcely glimpsed its full and glorious meaning for lost souls rescued by God incarnate, far transcending Mrs. Eddy's metaphysical abstractions.

My life-experience since coming to the Cross has followed the arc suggested by Lewis in a chapter title from the last of his Narnia stories: "Further Up and Further In." God's fourfold call on my life—politics, education, media, and ministry—has deepened and borne increasing fruit.

Walking in prayer together, Donna and I finally got marriage right. She gave her life to Christ a few years after I did. So did all three of our grown children, and now our grandson. A series of Presbyterian churches and parachurch ministries have blessed us with a strong spiritual sense of home and community.

We take every opportunity to witness of our faith to Christian Scientists, though receptivity is minimal. Sadly, few within our extended family on both sides have yet come to know the Lord.

We don't doubt, though, that the Hound of Heaven is tirelessly pursuing all of them even now, just as he pursued us. "The Lord is not willing that any should perish, but that all should come to repentance" (II Peter 3.9).

Where the path led for Carol Wilson and her daughters, I don't know. I'm sad to say that Mark Reed, with whom I am still in touch, left the church after encountering a personal crisis. He will always have a cherished place in my heart as the Ananias of my Christian conversion.

The Christian Science church and its prominent supporting institutions such as Principia and Adventure Unlimited remain on the scene, bravely fighting a slow decline. The wider sphere of self-salvation offerings has never been busier, though. As G.K. Chesterton observed, "When men choose not to believe in God, they do not thereafter believe in nothing, they become capable of believing in anything." Our times exactly.

Six Lessons

It took me well over a year to ponder out this narrative and get it in writing. Slow and steady. "First the blade, then the ear, after that the full corn in the ear," says Jesus (Mark 4:28).

Summing everything up in terms of lessons learned, here are half a dozen action points and attitudes, reminders to myself, that I'll offer to the reader as well.

1. ***Be encouraged.*** Jesus is constantly in pursuit of souls. There is unseen drama in every life, a contest for ultimate allegiance. Aslan is on the move.

2. ***Be ready.*** You may be called on as a link in the chain of someone's conversion to Christ, their own Ananias. The opportunity may never recur. Who needs you and when? Is it today?

3. ***Be introspective.*** The illusion that you can command yourself, sustain yourself, advance yourself, and save yourself (or be another's savior) takes many subtle forms. How is your heart haughty? Where are you vulnerable?

4. ***Be alert.*** The Hound of Heaven desires you and will not be denied. His design for you is a surrendered life, lifelong. Can you sense him near?

5. *Be insightful.* Have eyes to see. Self-salvation is the serpent's original lie and universal poison. False horizontal schemes for utopia are everywhere. The vertical power of the Cross defeats them all. There's a role for you. Don't miss it.

6. *Be bold.* Have a tongue to testify. Religion and politics and economics and technology and culture aren't separate things, but facets of one thing: the human condition called fallenness. Pray the Holy Spirit gives you vision and voice to attest the one and only answer: Christ and him crucified.

'Love Wist to Pursue'

There is much more that could be said about my story and its lessons. Why does self-salvation enthrall so many people in so many forms, despite its manifest bankruptcy? Why are spiritual counterfeits gaining in America and across the affluent West, even as spiritual truth in the person of Jesus Christ gains dramatically in the global South?

And here amongst us, what makes one person—myself, for example—susceptible to the pursuing Hound of Heaven when others all around him resist effortlessly and heedlessly, as it would seem?

I don't know the answer. But I pray daily that lost souls still fleeing him "down the arches of the years…down the labyrinthine ways of my own mind," as Francis Thompson puts it, will find that flight as futile as I did.[11]

---

[11] See poem in Appendix A, first stanza

May the poet's ultimate realization that "Fear wist not to evade as Love wist to pursue," played out so dramatically in my experience, become the experience of countless others as well.[12]

By the way, if you have not read "The Hound of Heaven" poem by Thompson, I urge you to set aside a little time, find the poem in the back pages here, and give it a try.

His 180 lines of florid and sometimes difficult Victorian verse, though exotic to contemporary tastes, will richly repay your effort. I'm betting it will grow on you as it has on me — a vivid retelling of the Greatest Story Ever Told.

And as seen in the hounding of my haughty heart by Jesus' relentless love, we're all invited to add our own episodes to the story. Indeed the rest of this book is but a long elaboration on that invitation.

Published in February 2016 as a booklet entitled,
"Jesus in Pursuit: The Hounding of a Haughty Heart"

[12] See poem in Appendix A, 2nd stanza

Pontius Pilate exhibits Jesus to the crowd (Dore)

CHAPTER 2:
WHAT SHALL I DO WITH JESUS WHO IS CALLED CHRIST?[13]

Actions speak louder than words. Christian Science claims to "adore Jesus" and "owe him endless homage."[14] Yet it refuses to worship him as the Son of God enthroned at the Father's right hand, the Messiah of whom we're taught in the Old and New Testaments and in historic Christianity across twenty centuries. The more I wrestled with this contradiction, the more it troubled me.

[13] Matthew 27:22

[14] SH 26:1 and 18:5

I THOUGHT I WAS A CHRISTIAN

"A man may honestly think himself honest, and a fresh week's experience may make him doubt it altogether," says a character in of George MacDonald's novels. "I sorely want a God to make me honest."

That was my situation exactly. I truly thought I was a Christian. I called myself one, and I most earnestly claimed to be a follower of Jesus Christ.

I tried to center my life on God as he did. I lived by his Sermon on the Mount and the Ten Commandments. I went to church every week and read the Bible every day. I ordered my thinking by the Lord's Prayer, even worked at healing by prayer after the Master's own example.

But I had never really come to know Jesus Christ. Not recognizing Jesus as God incarnate, how could I enthrone him as Lord in my heart? John's self held that throne.

Affirming my own perfection and denying sin, how could I receive Jesus as the loving Savior who died on the cross for me personally? John was in no need of saving.

Not knowing him to be alive, reigning at God's right hand, interceding for me, how could I receive the treasures he was ready to grant if I but asked them in his name? John prayed with logic, not petition.

Dismissing as superstitious those who are buried with him in baptism and raised with him in the eucharist of bread and wine, what part had I in the body of Christ? John thought himself part of a better and higher fellowship.

Presuming to read Scripture scientifically, which is to say selectively, how obedient was I to him who said his words will never pass away? John walked after a different leader.

Years of Wrestling

Yes, for a long time I thought I was a Christian, and it's true that sociologically I was more nearly that than anything else. But theologically I was unrecognizable to Paul and the believers at Antioch or to the Lord himself and his men from Galilee. He would have said sadly to me, "I never knew you" (Matthew 7:23).

I'm convinced, though, that he knows me very well now, for at last I have come to know him. Years spent wrestling with five simple questions rewarded me well. Those questions were:

- Who is Jesus Christ?

- Why have the ages worshipped him?

- What does he offer me?

- What does he demand of me?

- What is the cost of refusing him?

In searching the Scriptures for answers, I have found the one priceless pearl, Jesus my Savior and Lord, my best friend and elder brother.

To spend all my days adoring him, exalting him, serving him, and proclaiming him, and then to spend eternity companioning with him and shepherded by him, is finally my sense of what it means to be a Christian. What a discovery; what a joy. Thank you, Father.

Written in July 1997
to share with interested friends

WHAT TWO OF US
DECIDED TO DO

Dear Friend: Having in common with you a background as Christian Scientists, and after much prayer and searching of the Scriptures, we are writing to tell you about a transforming experience in our lives.

We want to explain what turned us from following Mary Baker Eddy and made us disciples of Jesus Christ. As such, these pages will probably be difficult reading for you.

But please consider our communication in the same spirit it was written, the spirit of meekness. We seek to "speak the truth in love," as God requires (Eph. 4:15). We pray you will be moved to action as a result.

Meeting Him Anew

Our experience was like that of the treasurer on the desert road in Acts (Acts 8:26-40). Or like that of the Baptist in the opening scene of John's gospel (John 1:29-34). We yearned, as they did, to understand God's promise of a man who would save the world.

We recognized ourselves as comparable to the warden at Philippi, devoted and dutiful but guilt-ridden almost to death (Acts 16:25-34). And though fired with godly zeal, like Saul heading to Damascus, we were as blind as he was to God's personal presence in our midst (Acts 9:1-22).

What reached us in this lost condition was just what reached each of them. It was the good news of Jesus, the Word made flesh, the crucified and risen Son of God incarnate.

Facing Our Flaws

The road to the Cross differed for each of us. But similar for all was a profound rethinking, a starting-over that was at first hesitant and then joyous. It began with facing up to what we honestly knew about ourselves as deeply flawed human beings.

The next step was opening up to what the New Testament actually says the answer is. Through this process we gradually saw that man's plight is more terrible, but God's provision more wonderful, than we had ever realized in many years of reading Mrs. Eddy.

We learned that Jesus is alive today, personally involved in our world, powerfully renewing and guiding the lives of those who let him do so. That his mission and destiny, identity and authority are spelled out in the Bible quite differently from what the weekly lesson-sermons portray. That he expects more of a commitment from every person, and desires more of a relationship with each one, than rationalism wants to admit.

What would you do if presented with this biblical evidence of a real and living Jesus, knocking for admission at the door of your heart? What each of us did was give ourselves to him, surrender to him as Savior and Lord, as humbly and completely as we could.

There came a day when some friend fearlessly and selflessly offered us the simple invitation that believers long ago gave the warden (and the treasurer, and the unseeing Saul): "Believe on the Lord Jesus Christ, and thou shalt be saved" (Acts 16:31). We accepted and we've never been the same. In brotherly concern, like Ananias coming to Saul, we now extend the invitation to you.

What Happened?

Deciding for Christ and choosing a denomination or church are two quite separate decisions. Only the first of those is our subject here. We're attesting that the reliability of Jesus is absolute. We hope you will find this out as we did. From there on, the reliability of *Science and Health* and its author is for you to judge.

We just know that it meant the world to us to have our eyes opened to the crucial missing words in the verse just quoted from Acts 16, a verse that Mrs. Eddy for some reason shortens to: "Believe…and thou shalt be saved" (SH 23:29). We don't think such use of altered quotations reflects well on a Bible textbook.

Please understand, though. We are not writing to attack Christian Science or to condemn its followers. For us to do that would be offensive and insulting. It would amount to a repudiation of our heritage, our parents and families, whole decades of our life stories. That is not the purpose of this letter, and we fervently hope it is not the effect.

Our purpose is simply to answer the question, "What happened to you?" Friends, relatives, and former church associates have asked us that in countless spoken or unspoken ways. Why the change in what we believe, where we worship, how we live? — they wanted to know.

We're replying now that the great happening in our lives, the reason for all those changes, is not a "what" but a "who." The reason is Jesus. He happened to us. We've found that having a relationship with Jesus, getting to know him, is the single greatest event and experience in life, bar none. He makes everything different.

We can tell you on the authority of Scripture and of our own life experience that Jesus lives, he cares, he loves you, he has a plan for you, and he is able to redeem you for a life that is new in every way. He will give you true peace, and a purpose for living that is far greater than anything you can think or imagine.

We can also tell you on the authority of Scripture, that if you receive Jesus as Lord and Savior, you will have eternal life, and that if you don't, you won't.

Our Sufficient Guide

You need not take our word for it, of course. You shouldn't, on a matter of this ultimate importance. Much better that you should examine the Scriptures for answers to these issues. Mrs. Eddy characterized herself and her students as "adherents of Truth, [who] take the inspired Word of the Bible as our sufficient guide to eternal Life" (SH 497:3). Where in fact does that guide take you?

To find out, we urge you to search the Scriptures systematically and honestly, and with personal discipline. See what the Bible says are the answers, and write down your findings. You can decide later whether or not you accept these answers. The first step is just to determine what the Bible itself is telling us.

We also suggest that you focus on what all the Bible says about these questions, and not take isolated verses to get your answer. For example, we suggest you read the entire book of John, seeking light on the issues of sin and salvation, prophecy and fulfillment, and above all, the promised Messiah. Who is he, and why does it matter to us today? Make note of the specific verses that speak to these issues. Later, you can review these notes to check for accuracy.

A seeker who does take on the Gospel of John might ask: What does this book say about Jesus? Who is he? Who does Jesus say he is? Who do his friends say he is? What do his enemies say about him? What do the neutral people who meet Jesus have to say about him? Who does Jesus claim to be? What does Jesus say is his purpose for coming into the world?

In our seeking, these points were made clear in the text: that Jesus is the Son of God, that he came into the world to save sinners, that he is the Lamb of God who is slain to be the payment for our sins, and that he claims to be the Lord, to be God incarnate.

The seeker might next ask: What does all of this biblical information imply for me? What does it mean in terms of my personal response? In the words of Pontius Pilate: "What shall I do then with Jesus, who is called Christ?" (Matthew 27:22)

What will you do with Jesus? Each of us, confronted with this question, was led to acknowledge that Jesus Christ is Lord, that he has the supreme claim to govern each aspect of our lives, and that we are called to place our faith in him, and to worship and obey him. Having chosen to do this, we found him to be our one true Friend, our Savior, our comfort and hope.

He loves us, and he loves you. We are confident that if you honestly and openly examine Scripture, you will conclude as we have, that Jesus is who he says he is, and that he will do for you as he has done for us—to purchase our salvation at the cost of his own life, and to give us eternal life.

Written that You May Believe

In your search of the Scriptures, we suggest you do this in two parts. First, ask the question, "What does the Bible say?" Here we have found the use of restatement to be particularly helpful; that is, restating in your own words what the Bible says in a particular passage.

Next, examine your restatement along with the Scripture passage, and decide whether or not the message articulated in Scripture is true, and whether you are prepared to believe it. As you carefully study the Gospel of John, you may find it helpful to consider the author's stated purpose for writing his recollections: "[T]hese are written that you may believe that Jesus is the Christ, and that by believing you may have life in his name" (John 20:31).

His book did fulfill its purpose in our experience. Another New Testament book—any of the gospels, or one of Paul's letters such as Romans or Colossians—would have done as well. We examined Scripture, considered the claims of Jesus Christ, and decided to put our trust and faith in him.

We have chosen to follow Jesus because we believe he is all that he claims to be, the light of the world, our Savior and our Lord, the one with the power to forgive sins, to grant us eternal life, to give us fellowship with the Father, and the one with sole and exclusive right to govern our entire lives. We have placed him in control of our lives and committed ourselves to live in obedience to him.

We believe that if you honestly examine what the Bible says about Jesus Christ, you will come to the same conclusion we did. When you do, you will have a powerful decision to make: "What shall I do with Jesus, who is called Christ?"

Will you receive him, will you accept him and surrender your life to him? Or will you reject him, and refuse him the authority that is rightfully his? Will you be content to learn about him? Or will you really get to know him, just as he already knows you?

There are no more important questions in anyone's life than these. We pray God will richly bless you as you wrestle with them.

Co-authored with my friend Carl Gans (1949-2011)
and published in 2000 as our welcome letter
on the Ananias website

ONCE BLIND, NOW SEEING

What a shock to hear a story about someone coldly defying God, and suddenly realize the story is about me. I have a sense of how King David must have felt when confronted with his destructive selfishness (II Samuel 12:7).

Recently in studying Luke 20, where Jesus tells of the vineyard tenants brutalizing the owner's messengers one after another and finally killing his son, it hit me that this had been my pattern of behavior when following Christian Science for many years.

Following Mrs. Eddy, I obstinately ignored the Old Testament's repeated witness of sin, salvation, and prophecy — and then climaxed my obstinacy by rejecting the New Testament's good news that Jesus Christ had come as God incarnate to rescue me for life eternal under his authority.

"This is the heir: come, let us kill him, that the inheritance may be ours," says fallen humanity when the beloved son arrives (Luke 20:14).

Mulish

True, Christian Science doesn't explicitly say this. But in denying Jesus' divinity and his vicarious atonement for us on the cross,

Mrs. Eddy's followers set the Lord at naught, usurp his authority, and enthrone themselves in his place — "that the inheritance [sinful mortals self-reconciled with a holy God] may be ours."

So when I read in Hebrews 6:4-6 of the sad condition of those who, after having had so many advantages of God's grace, still "crucify to themselves the Son of God afresh, and put him to an open shame," it becomes very personal. I feel myself convicted of a long mulish intransigence during all those years in the gospel-denying Christian Science movement. As Nathan told David: "Thou art the man" (II Samuel 12:7).

Even with millennia of the Father's patience and forbearance from the time of Abraham to that of Abraham Lincoln, even with 66 books of Holy Scripture proclaiming true truth on every page, somehow the Boston prophetess and her adoring throng could still miss the way and exalt their intellectual pride over Christ's sacrificial humility.

Somehow my own family and so many other Principians could presume to claim the saints' inheritance on no terms but their own. Somehow —

It makes me more grateful than ever for the "amazing grace that saved a wretch like me — once blind, but now I see."

Published in December 2019
on the Ananias website

TO KNOW ONLY CHRIST
CRUCIFIED

"To the Son of God alone faith ought to look. On him it relies. In him it rests and terminates. If it proceed farther, it will disappear, and will no longer be faith, but a delusion."

That's from John Calvin in his *Commentary on Ephesians*. He adds: "Let us remember that true faith confines its view so entirely to Christ that it neither knows, nor desires to know, anything else."

Calvin is but paraphrasing St. Paul, who writes in I Corinthians 2:2, "I determined not to know anything among you, save Jesus Christ, and him crucified."

Though Mrs. Eddy twice quotes this text (SH 39:7 & 200:25), in practice she defied it. Her whole thrust in Christian Science is to proceed farther than Jesus the Son of God — to look beyond him into a higher metaphysics that ultimately supersedes faith or belief with privileged, perfect knowing, what the Greeks called *gnosis*.

Eddy's promethean ambition to blend the Gospel of Calvary with the mind science of Quimby is an example of the fallacy C.S. Lewis called "Christianity and" — any newfangled religious offshoot that tries to graft human self-salvation schemes onto the sole salvation of the Cross. (See *The Screwtape Letters*, Chapter 25.)

No verse in the Bible has been more utterly life-changing for me than I Corinthians 2:2. Stumbling across this Scripture in my thirties, starting to wonder what life would be like if I humbly obeyed it, and recognizing with growing disquiet how massively Mrs. Eddy disobeyed it, played a key role in freeing me from her grip.

Yet even today I catch myself approaching life's challenges from the unwitting standpoint of "Christianity and [fill in the blank]." Take a mental inventory of your own and you will see how insidious the temptation is. Paul himself must have been susceptible to it, or he wouldn't have avowed himself "determined" not to deviate, in that letter to the church at Corinth.

What's our best protection from the fatal mistake Calvin warned of, looking past the Son of God so that faith disappears into delusion? It is constantly and steadfastly "looking unto Jesus the author and finisher of our faith" (Hebrews 12:2).

Published in March 2016
on the Ananias website

READY TO ENTHRONE HIM?

Ten of us who serve as elders at my Presbyterian church were stationed around the sanctuary after today's sermon to pray with anyone who wanted to accept or renew a saving relationship with Jesus Christ.

What a sacred privilege that was for me, a onetime Christian Scientist once smugly indifferent to any such relationship. Here is the simple prayer I asked individuals to say aloud with me:

- Jesus Son of God, my selfishness and sin have separated me far from God your Father, and I am powerless to save myself.

- Please bring me near him again through your death and resurrection.

- I give myself to you as Savior and Lord. I put you on the throne of my life from now on.

The sermon text was the Apostle's succinct proclamation of the Gospel in I Peter 3:18: "Christ also suffered once for sins, the righteous for the unrighteous, to bring you to God. He was put to death in the body but made alive in the Spirit."

Our sin problem and its solution through the Cross, as presented in this verse and in my prayer at church this morning, are so distorted gnostically and metaphysically by Christian Science that all of it would have meant nothing to me before the Lord Jesus crashed into my life forty years ago.

Now it means everything to me — as it does to the new and old believers who came forward to bow with us today. No more self-salvation. King Jesus on the throne. New birth and a whole new life to live. What a joy!

It might be that you, the person reading this right now, wherever you are and whatever your circumstances, find yourself ready at this very moment to enthrone Jesus in your own heart of hearts. Possible, perhaps?

If you want to take that step, why not do so here and now? Why wait any longer to be reborn in Him? All it takes is to say that little prayer and mean it.

It doesn't involve getting down on your knees, or telling anyone, or finding a new church, or dropping Christian Science without a backward glance.

All of those can come later. Today it just involves saying the prayer. Honestly, what's stopping you?

Published in July 2019
on the Ananias website

St. Jerome translating the Bible, 382 AD (Durer)

CHAPTER 3:
WHAT IF THE BIBLE IS ITS OWN KEY?

As a follower of Christian Science, I accepted that the true meaning of Holy Scripture had gone undiscovered through many centuries until Mrs. Eddy's time. Then it struck me: Would a loving God have kept his people in the dark that way for so long? Maybe no "Key to the Scriptures" was needed to unlock the Bible's life-giving message after all. Perhaps nothing had been locked shut but my own proud heart.

LOCKED OUT NO MORE

Thinking about the beautiful, life-giving truths we find in the New Testament, and the strange way in which they were hidden from me for the first half of my life — hidden in plain sight — I was struck by an eerie analogy.

Suppose you were persuaded to buy a wonderful-sounding new kind of key that would not only unlock your house, but also operate your car, and even open your safe-deposit box. One key for everything. What a benefit.

But by some awful mistake or cruel trick, when you tried it, the key was all wrong. It worked backwards, so that your now your front door was locked tighter than ever, your car would not start, nor could you get into the safe-deposit box.

Worse yet, by a sort of hypnotic effect you actually thought those valuables from the box were in your hands when they weren't, you were driving along toward your destination instead of standing still, and you were inside and warm at home instead of locked out on your doorstep in the cold.

Wrong Key

Not what a benefit, but what a cheat, right? And what a trap, because you could be stuck there forever, relying on the wrong key, unless someone came along to snap you out of the illusion of false comfort and security.

This is the cheat, perhaps well-intended but disastrous all the same, that Mary Baker Eddy's misnamed Key to the Scriptures, *Science and Health*, and the Christian Science religion derived from it, impose on anyone who follows them.

Her false key excludes the follower from his only true home in time and eternity, a saving knowledge of Jesus Christ as God incarnate. It deceives him that he is getting somewhere spiritually, though really mired in self-salvation. And it deludes him that he has found eternal riches, the pearl of great price.

Such was my lost and confused situation as a devoted Christian Scientist until well into my forties. I started Sunday school at age five, joined the Mother Church at 15, received all my education at Principia, took class instruction at 28, and became the reader in my branch church at 34. Meanwhile I was working as executive director of Adventure Unlimited, the international Christian Science youth organization.

The "someone" who came along to snap me out of it was Jesus Christ himself. My encounter with him as Savior and Lord built to a climax over a period of years, gradually convicting me through various individuals, experiences, and books—among them the New Testament gospels and letters.

Published in July 2015
on the Ananias website

TO HAVE THE MIND OF CHRIST

For many years I faithfully joined other Christian Scientists in promising to "watch, and pray for that Mind to be in us which was also in Christ Jesus." But that reference to a verse from Philippians, found in the Sixth Tenet of Christian Science (SH 497:24), never came alive for me in all its gospel meaning.

Misled by Mrs. Eddy, I simply took it as one more way of describing the "metaphysical work" that she asked of us: knowing the truth, denying error, claiming dominion, reflecting God's intelligence.

Only after coming to the Cross did I realize that Paul in this passage is not talking about such common, human efforts at self-salvation. Not at all. He's talking about the uniquely divine combination of self-emptying ("Thy will, not mine," Matthew 26:39) and self-proclaimed authority ("you will see the Son of Man sitting on the right hand of power," Matthew 26:64) that Jesus alone, as God incarnate, could have manifested and then made available to you and me.

No Reputation

"That mind which was also in Christ Jesus" (Philippians 2:5) isn't truly understood unless we take in the whole context of Philippians 2:1-11, especially verses 6-8:

> Who, being in the form of God, thought it not robbery to be equal with God: But made himself of no reputation, and took upon him the form of a servant, and was made in the likeness of men: And being found in fashion as a man, he humbled himself, and became obedient unto death, even the death of the cross.

I don't ever remember seeing those explanatory lines about Jesus' attitude, mentality, or state of mind — or the next three verses about the Father's consequent exaltation of the Son, and the worship we therefore owe him — in a Christian Science lesson-sermon or periodical. Ever.

Checking the Bible my wife had used for over twenty years to study the weekly lesson, marked with blue chalk, I found this confirmed. The faint blue haze that remains on a passage marked even once, was not there. That part of the page is pristine white. Nor are these six verses quoted anywhere in Mary Baker Eddy's published writings.

And no wonder, since the Scientists' contention that Jesus was not God — a contention seen even in the vague, evasive wording of Tenets 2, 4, and 5, just ahead of the vow to "watch and pray" in Tenet 6 — is directly contradicted by Philippians 2:6-11.

So that passage *must* go unmentioned. It wouldn't do to start Mrs. Eddy's followers wondering why her church disregards the command that "every knee should bow" and "every tongue should confess that Jesus Christ is Lord."

I am grateful that now as his unreserved disciple, my knee and my tongue are joyfully under that discipline. And you?

Published in May 2012
on the Ananias website

TO KEEP FAITH WITH PAUL

When I initially left the Christian Science church and received Christian baptism, years ago, I regarded Mary Baker Eddy as a well-intentioned spiritual seeker who got some crucial things wrong but was still in some ways a reliable spiritual guide.

In time, however, I came to believe that she was willfully false to Scripture and no true disciple of Jesus Christ, hence not someone we should follow in any way.

Recently in studying St. Paul's letter to the Galatians, I was reminded of two glaring examples of Mrs. Eddy's unreliable exegesis. One occurs at the head of Chapter VII on page 107 in her textbook, *Science and Health*, where she quotes in reference to herself, Galatians 1:11,12:

> I certify you, brethren, that the gospel which was preached of me is not after man. For I neither received it of man, neither was I taught it, but by the revelation of Jesus Christ.

Yet Paul in this very passage has just warned against the attractions of "another gospel [which] would pervert the gospel of

Jesus Christ." And what else is the Mrs. Eddy doctrine, with its denial of Jesus' divinity and his atoning death, but exactly that?

The dishonest quoting recurs on page 478 of *Science and Health*, where she again claims the mantle of a modern-day Paul with these lines from Galatians 1:15,16: "But when it pleased God, who separated me from my mother's womb, and called me by his grace…I conferred not with flesh and blood."

Wait a minute, though. Open your Bible and look closely at the words she omitted with those three dots: "to reveal his Son in me, that I might preach him among the heathen."

What can we do with this, other than to conclude that Mrs. Eddy did *not* see her mission as bearing witness for the Son of God incarnate and preaching faithfully of that crucified and risen Lord? Rather it was her own quasi-biblical metaphysics that she sought to advance.

To say that Mary Baker Eddy, in these and many similar passages from her writings, used questionable interpretations or played loose with the Bible, is too kind, I'm afraid. She played *false* with the Bible.

This seems to me an utter forfeiture of our trust. How does it seem to you?

Published in November 2012
on the Ananias website

TO ACT WITH THE APOSTLES

How did Jesus' crucifixion and resurrection utterly transform human experience and change the world forever?

By convincing a few dozen of his followers, who then convinced billions down the centuries and around the world, that

Jesus was God incarnate and that through his blood believers could enter into eternal life.

This is what jumps off the pages of the Book of Acts if you carefully read its early chapters, as I did recently during Holy Week.

What's not there is any hint of Mary Baker Eddy's metaphysical version of reality, "perfect God and perfect man" as posited in her "Key to the Scriptures" (SH 259:13). No trace.

I would challenge anyone who is wondering whether to continue following Christian Science, simply to study Acts 1-9 with fresh eyes and see if they find there any support for such familiar contentions of Mrs. Eddy and *Science and Health* as these:

- That man is perfect and not really a sinner.

- That Jesus only seemed to have died on the cross.

- That Christ and Jesus are not one and the same person.

- That after the ascension Jesus' human identity ceased to exist.

- That the Holy Spirit or Comforter didn't come to us until 1866.

- That Christian healing requires a "scientific statement of being" to be fully effective.

- That God's revelation of himself and his salvation plan in New Testament times was anything less than final (SH 107:5).

A fair-minded reader will find St. Luke's account in Acts teaching just the opposite in every case. Remember how Mrs. Eddy invites the inquirer to "ascertain for yourself if the author has given you the correct interpretation of Scripture" (SH 547:7)? Very well then, try it.

I wish someone had dared me to look over these initial chapters of Acts and compare them with the false gospel of *Science and Health*, some time in the first forty years of my life when I was under the spell of Christian Science. I would have come to the Cross far sooner.

Published in April 2020
on the Ananias website

COMBATING THE ENEMY

Satan's destructive intentions for us and his deadly struggle against Jesus were never made clear to me in forty years of studying Christian Science, though they are evident throughout the Bible.

The Enemy under his many names and disguises, from the serpent in Genesis to the dragon in Revelation, is mentioned often in Mrs. Eddy's writings, but only to be explained away. She posits "the nothingness of evil" (SH 563:17) and the "unreality of sin" (SH 461:26), then goes on to equate Satan, the devil, and demons with evil or sin. End of subject.

After quoting Jesus' specific warning for us to "fear him who is able to destroy both soul and body in hell" (Matthew 10:28), she says this means to beware of sin, not Satan (SH 196:15). Satan she has already dismissed a few pages earlier as an "illusive personification" (SH 187:11). His works too are "illusion," she writes (Mis. 68:16). "The existence of one personal devil" is but baseless "supposition," she asserts, "evil beliefs" and nothing more (Mis. 191:21, 29).

I have concluded, however, after studying Scripture on its own terms and setting Mrs. Eddy's books aside, that explaining-away can only abet the Enemy's prime objective of lulling us into thinking he does not exist.

"Let us alone" was the unclean spirit's plea to Jesus in the first miracle ascribed to him in the first gospel written about him (Mark 1:24). The Lord did not oblige and neither should we. His example of personally addressing the demons ("devils" in the King James translation) and their chief, Satan, from a position not of weakness but of God-given strength, must be followed if Christian Scientists or any of us really want to access divine power as he did.

I was recently asked by Mick, a Christian I correspond with in prison, to look into God's Word for precepts that could help him in battling what he calls the demons of bipolar mental illness. He said that after a difficult period, the medications were finally stabilizing him, but he wanted to go deeper and win the spiritual battle behind his physical and mental torment.

"I've been studying about demons, but not understanding much of it," Mick wrote. "Please give me your understanding with references, from which I might get more insight." After a lot of research and prayer, I came up with ten points, each clearly supported (it seems to me) by one or more texts.

Power Against Demons

1. Satan is strong, but God is stronger. (Gen. 3:15, Job 1:6-12, Mt. 4:1-11, Lk. 11:14-20)

2. We must be always watchful and active, because Satan's agents, the demons or devils, are constantly attacking us. (Mt. 10:24-28, Lk. 11:21-26, Lk. 22:24-34, I Pet. 5:6-11)

3. In believing on God's Son, Jesus, we receive power to cast out demons. (Mt. 10:8, Mk. 16:17, Lk. 10:17-20)

4. To use that power, we must stay close to Jesus through unwavering faith, prayer, and fasting. The power is never ours personally, nor can we dare use it selfishly or carelessly. (Mk. 9:17-29, Lk. 10:17-20, Acts 8:9-24, Acts 19:13-16)

5. Demon possession is never God's will. It is not anyone's natural or normal or permanent condition. Satan's final defeat in the end times (Isa. 14:12-15, Mt. 25:41, Rev. 12:7-11) is preceded by our victories here and now over him and his demons. (Lk. 8:26-39, Lk.13:10-17)

6. As we were originally made in God's image, and as we are now redeemed in Christ, our normal and natural condition is to companion with angels, not demons. (Mt. 4:1-11, Mt. 26:47-54)

7. Satan and his demons use lies, deceptions, and disguises, even false applications of Scripture, in the attempt to trap us and kill us. (Mt. 4:1-11, John 8:31-50, II Cor. 11:14) But God in Christ provides us full armor for defense and offense against every demon weapon or trick. (Eph. 6:10-18)

8. Satan and his demons know they will be defeated if identified and confronted. So they seek to be concealed, ignored, or bargained with. (II Cor. 11:14, Mk. 1:23, 24, Lk. 8:26-28) We can prevail by addressing them directly and with authority, as Jesus did. (Mk. 1:25-27, Lk. 8:29-33, Mt. 16:23)

9. Our troubles including sin, sickness, suffering, or sorrow are sometimes the indirect result of a fallen world and other times the direct result of demon attack. But

since Satan originally caused the Fall and since he still constantly seeks our destruction, we can always be helped by coming against him in Jesus' name, and we must not cease doing so. There is no neutrality: if we are not firmly on Christ's side, we will be pulled to the Enemy's side. (Mt. 16:23, Lk. 22:3-6, 24-34)

10. With each victory over Satan and his demons, there comes a great increase in our joy of life and our usefulness to others, in service to God's purposes. (Mk.16:9, Lk. 8:35-39, Lk. 22:32, Acts 8:9-24)

Such was the outline I sent to my friend in the penitentiary. I've since seen Mick make great strides toward victory over the demons of mental illness. It led to his self-mastery and usefulness for the Kingdom — already greatly advanced since his conversion behind bars four years ago — advancing further still.

Published in November 2008
on the Ananias website

CONTESTING FOR TRUTH

Mary Baker Eddy invites us to put her and her book to the test, "and so ascertain if the author has given you the correct interpretation of Scripture" (SH 547:7). We should do just that, with our eyes wide open to the divergence between the two books at many points.

Either *Science and Health* must correct the Bible, or the Bible must correct Eddy's textbook. They can't both be true throughout. Let me offer a case study.

Jesus Pushed Aside

A few pages back, in "To Keep Faith with Paul," I briefly took issue with how Mrs. Eddy handles four verses in Paul's letter to the Galatians. Now let's take a closer look at what she did to this important book, a document that has been called has been called the first autobiography of a Christian convert. The verses in question were these:

> I certify you, brethren, that the gospel which is preached of me is not after man, for I neither received it of man, neither was I taught it, but by the revelation of Jesus Christ…. But when it pleased God, who separated me from my mother's womb, and called me by his grace, to reveal his Son in me, that I might preach him among the heathen, immediately I conferred not with flesh and blood (Galatians 1:11, 12, 15, 16).

I mentioned that we find the first two verses quoted verbatim on SH 107 as an epigraph to her chapter on "Science, Theology, and Medicine," and the other two quoted in part on SH 478, in her "Recapitulation" chapter — which we're told grew out of an early writing that became the nucleus of her entire textbook as now received (see SH 465).

Significantly and typically, in citing Galatians 1:15, 16, Eddy omits Paul's key thought beginning at "to reveal" and ending at "heathen," thus obscuring his Christological point in order to make her own epistemological point about the question at hand, "Is there intelligence in matter?"

Her answer to that question occupies the next several pages, a thousand words or so, and quotes the New Testament three more times, all without ever once mentioning Jesus or Christ. Such proof-texting, always to the detriment of our Lord's true identity and work, is sadly characteristic of *Science and Health* from beginning to end.

As for Eddy's initial citation from this important passage in Galatians, verses 1:11 and 1:12, one marvels at the presumptuousness of an author who could claim to be preaching the identical gospel that Paul did, a message allegedly taught to her (as it had been to him) "by the revelation of Jesus Christ"—and who yet could build her whole book and system on deconstructing every element of Paul's core message "that Christ died for our sins according to the Scriptures" (I Cor. 15:3).

To divert for a moment to my own spiritual autobiography, from Paul's, it's unforgettable how a breakthrough in my reassessment of the claims of Christian Science occurred when the work of serving as a reader in our branch church prompted me to start reading the Bible chapter by chapter instead of verse by verse, "lesson-sermon style."

What the Chalk Left Out

One eye-opener was noticing how the blue-chalk residue (from the lesson-sermon markers we used) on so many pages tended to fall upon the same few passages, effectively walling off the compliant Christian Science student from vast parts of God's word in Scripture.

Another eye-opener was realizing how frequently the context of a chapter in its entirety (especially in the New Testament) would redirect—or sometimes even reverse—the implication of some shorter passage the lessons or periodicals had lifted out of context and misleadingly presented as "truth."

Again and again, that redirection took the form of impressing on me the very gospel Paul summarizes in his great Corinthians declaration just now quoted: that I was a sinner in need of a savior, that the Savior was here, the God-man named Jesus, and that we must accept no substitutes.

I mention this because the warning to accept no substitutes is exactly what we find in reading the whole chapter in the case of Galatians 1.

Backing up from verse 11, in which Mrs. Eddy dishonestly (there is no gentler way to put it) wraps herself on SH 107, what do we encounter? This emphatic statement in Galatians 1:8:

"Though we, or an angel from heaven, preach any other gospel unto you than that which we have preached unto you, let him be accursed."

Further Questions

It couldn't be any clearer — and it couldn't reflect any more unfavorably on Mrs. Eddy, by whom so many of us were taught that we're not really sinners, Jesus isn't really God, he didn't really die on the cross, the Bible isn't really inerrant, and so much more.

I will stop there. But notice how many other lines of inquiry abound from these two conflicting passages in Jesus' book, the Bible, and Eddy's book, *Science and Health.*

- We could ask, apropos Galatians 1:6, how so many Christians who should have known better were lured away from the grace of Christ into the self-salvation of Christian Science from the 1870s down to the 1930s and beyond.

- We could ask, apropos Galatians 1:10, how much of that allure was a matter of Mrs. Eddy's ego-pleasing blandishments to her followers in the form of a) flattery that coos "You're perfect" and b) creature-comforts that promise "You're healed."

- We could ask, apropos the first eight lines on page 547 of *Science and Health*, by what leap of logic anyone can claim that a) the airtight coherence of every statement in the textbook, and b) the monopolistic superiority of Eddyism over any other kind of Christian prayer, are both "proved" by those scattered healings that result from Christian Science prayer.

All this we can take up some other time. For now, we should end as we began: facing squarely the impossibility that both the Bible and *Science and Health*, his book and hers, can be all true — since they explicitly contradict each other.

Only one of the two books can be of God. Not both. My vote is with Holy Scripture.

Published in March 2017
on the Ananias website

FINDING THE TRUE BREAD

Do you have a lifetime theme verse from the Bible? Reflecting on this is a way of seeing into your spiritual autobiography, the arc of what God is doing with your life story. Our pastor recently asked about mine, and I realized there are two that stand out.

One of my life verses is from the Beatitudes, Jesus' words in Matthew 5:8: "Blessed are they which do hunger and thirst after righteousness, for they shall be filled."

My path from Christian Science to the Cross some years ago was marked by the realization that Mrs. Eddy's teachings are not the bread of life (Isaiah 55:2), whereas Jesus himself is that true bread (John 6:35).

Since then I have learned that the hungering for Him, followed by the being filled by Him, isn't just a one-time process but a lifelong quest, an ever-rising cycle of discovery and growth.

Secret of the Lord

My other life verse is less often quoted but precious to me. Again from Jesus, this time in John 7:17: "If any man will do His [the Father's] will, he shall know of the doctrine, whether it be of God, or whether I speak of myself."

This came to my attention from C.S. Lewis's conversion story in *Surprised by Joy*, where he says near the end of Chapter XIV: "Really, a young Atheist cannot guard his faith too carefully. Dangers lie in wait for him on every side. You must not do, you must not even try to do, the will of the Father unless you are prepared to 'know of the doctrine.'"[15]

I've realized that my experience somewhat paralleled Lewis's, though I was coming not from atheism but from a semi-Scriptural belief system in which obeying God was encouraged and "knowing the doctrine" that Jesus died to save sinners like me was strictly discouraged. It turned out, in my case at least, the two couldn't be kept separate.

As Psalm 25:14 has it, "The secret of the Lord is with them that fear Him; and He will shew them His covenant." Show me he did — and what a surprise of joy to be let in on the (open) secret of Jesus Christ at last!

So again I ask: What's your lifetime theme verse, and why?

The true bread awaits you. Or as the writer of Hebrews put it with a different metaphor: "The word of God is quick and powerful and sharper than any two-edged sword, piercing even to the dividing asunder of soul and spirit, and of the joints and marrow" (4:12). Handle with care!

Published in August 2015
on the Ananias website

---

[15] Lewis makes a similar point in Chapter XII of the same book, specifically with reference to God's "unscrupulous…traps" awaiting the unbeliever who ventures to read G.K. Chesterton and George MacDonald, two of his favorite writers by whom I was also much influenced.

Birth of the church on Pentecost (Dore)

CHAPTER 4:
A GLORIOUS CHURCH, HOLY AND PERFECT?[16]

The Mary Baker Eddy organization claimed to welcome thinkers, yet it frowned on members thinking for themselves.[17] Though talking much of love, it made no allowance for the human heart. Aspiring to be "a church without creeds,"[18] it cut members off from the God-man, Jesus Christ, and staked all on one woman's assertions. Where did this leave Jesus' apostolic church, the central institution of history? I needed to find out.

[16] Ephesians 5:27, J.B. Phillips translation

[17] SH vii:13

[18] *Manual* 17:3

NO JESUS, NO CHURCH

How can there not be one word about Jesus in a newspaper story marking 100 years of worship services for a Denver-area church of Christ, Scientist — an article hundreds of words long and written by a well-regarded Christian Science practitioner?

One fears that the members of such a church, presenting themselves before the Lord at the end times, may well receive his stern dismissal, "I never knew you" (Matthew 7:23).

The March 27, 2008, *Denver Post* piece marks the centennial of First Church of Christ, Scientist, Littleton, Colorado, a month before. It makes mention of the Bible, the Lord's Prayer, "God's goodness," "God's benevolent laws," "God's constant presence and power," "spiritual ideas," "spiritual growth," and "spiritual renewal," and "Christian healing…through prayer" — but there is not a single mention of Jesus Christ.

One person and one only is named: "the woman who discovered Christian Science, Mary Baker Eddy." Her name, interestingly, is also the only thing in the story to appear in boldface type.

Marginalized

James Meyer, C.S., who authored the piece, is known to me as a godly man with many years of experience in the healing practice as well as lengthy service as Christian Science Committee on Publication for Colorado.

In the latter position, Meyer had to publish and speak constantly on the church's behalf for the information of the general public, so the absence of Jesus' name from his article is unlikely to be inadvertent.

No, that omission reflects all too accurately the marginalized position of the Savior in the theology and lives of Christian Scientists.

It was the desire to have the Lord Jesus at the center of our lives and theology that led me and my fellow sponsors of the Ananias website out of Christian Science and up to the foot of the Cross.

We soon found our individual commitment to him, in lieu of Mrs. Eddy, causing us to seek out a collective commitment to the body of believers identified not with her church but with his, "the church of the living God, the pillar and ground of the truth" (I Timothy 3:15).

And we continue to pray that every Christian Scientist will in the fullness of time reach the same life-transforming realization we did—the realization that the only true church is Jesus' church.

Published in April 2008
on the Ananias website

WHAT THEY'RE MISSING

"Church group takes dramatic turn." That recent headline in our local paper caught my attention. Then I really took notice when it developed the article was about something out of the ordinary occurring at the downtown Christian Science Reading Room near Denver's fashionable Larimer Square. Just how dramatic a turn might this be, I wondered.

The religion beat reporter who wrote the piece is good. We became friendly acquaintances years ago. Jean is quietly devout in her Catholic faith (not wanting readers' knowledge of it to color their view of what she writes), politically centrist, gracious, impeccably fair. I read on with confidence that her story, whatever it might be, would be honest and perceptive.

The news here, one learned, was that the committee chairman, someone named Nan, was innovatively fostering a discussion series which, in the reporter's words, doesn't just "stay true to founder Mary Baker Eddy's idea" of a reading room but seeks to be "more relevant" in a way "Eddy would approve of."

Such risk-taking in Christian Science church work isn't uncommon, but making a success of it when the backlash comes, is. The innovator moves ahead hopefully but warily, uncertain as to (a) what stir this may cause internally and (b) what difference it will make, internally or externally.

The so-what question came to mind when I saw on how bland and shallow a level the chairman's discussion experiment was proceeding. A premise for the relevance of it all, Nan told Jean, was that "these people, in biblical times, were busy too." Hardly a scoop worth stopping the presses.

Mary and Martha

Revealing in the same vein, and sadly typical of the Christless Christianity and self-salvation that Mrs. Eddy's followers are stuck with, was the story's final paragraph, where "the Mary and Martha problem" is trivialized (by the Christian Scientist being interviewed, not the reporter) to merely "finding serenity in a frantic world." As if the Savior of us all was merely advising the two sisters on time management.

If the session ever brought out Jesus' commendation of Mary for choosing "the better part" and attentively centering on Him, there's no evidence in this account from a discerning and careful journalist. On the contrary, it seems to have been Martha's misplaced priorities, works righteousness, and assertive indignation that "several [participants] related to" in the occasion's "eureka moment." And so much for the eternal issues at stake in Luke 10:38-42.

My friend Jean's skills as a reporter shone in bringing to light this key insight: "What several participants said they're missing from the world is a better sense of the Bible." Remarkable, isn't it, when Scientists study the Bible so faithfully every day and hear it read at length (more length than most evangelical churches, to be sure) twice a week in church.

But in those church readings there is still something missing, a participant named Laura remarked to Jean. More "continuity," not just snippets and short takes, is what another participant, Sue, said she hopes the reading room discussions will provide that other group settings for local Christian Science church members don't.

These good folks and seeking hearts may get more than they bargained for. It was the restless search for that something-missing, the quest for continuity in Scripture as provided by its supreme hero, the crucified and risen Lord Jesus, that led me *out* of Christian Science and to the foot of His cross.

When that kind of "eureka" begins to happen for more and more individuals, and next for small groups like the one described in the reading room article—and it will, here and there it already is—then we will really see the fulfillment of the so-far overly excited headline: "Church group takes dramatic turn."

Published in September 2007
on the Ananias website

MY MORNING MEAL

Does the morning quiet time with Scriptural readings and prayer, so beloved to many Christian Scientists, go away when you leave the practice and congregational life of Science to become a biblical Christian? It needn't and shouldn't. The solution our family found is but one of many that are available. Here's a glimpse of it.

Today with Easter approaching, my wife and I and our son all worked from a Bible study plan that included Matthew 26, Psalm 55, Lamentations 3, and I Corinthians 11 ("As often as ye do eat this bread, and drink this cup, ye do show the Lord's death till he come"). Tomorrow we'll be given a fresh but related group of Scriptures to read and pray over.

The study outline is based on the time-honored lectionaries of major Christian denominations, taking one through the whole Bible every two years. It's given in a little periodical we have discovered: the *Daily Devotional Guide*, published four times a year by the Fellowship of St. James, an ecumenical alliance of traditional Protestants, Catholics, and Orthodox.

At their website one can also find the *Daily Reflections* online study notes by Patrick Reardon, a fine Bible scholar, and links to their two excellent magazines on Christianity and culture, *Touchstone* and *Salvo*.

For over forty years I faithfully and (as I then thought) fruitfully read each day the Bible lessons in the *Christian Science Quarterly*. But when at last I realized the *Science and Health* portion of those readings was not just diluting but distorting and falsifying the biblical Word of God, I quit studying those "lesson-sermons." Nor have I missed them, either on weekdays or on Sundays.

Prayer and Study

Because I've been grateful for a couple of decades now, to have in place of them this alternative, and theologically sound, quarterly study guide from the Fellowship of St. James. As for daily prayer, it takes a number of forms throughout each day for Donna and me, from first waking to last words before sleep.

Specifically in connection with morning Bible study, I have devised, with the help of friends and mentors, a set formal prayer to say before starting the day's reading, and another to say upon concluding.

The prayer life of Christians who follow Jesus as Savior and Lord tends to vary, with some churches inclined to praise and petition God in spontaneous free-form expressions and others preferring set forms. (Classic examples of the latter include the Catholic Missal and the Anglican Book of Common Prayer.)

Donna and I and our three children — who all found their way from Christian Science to the Cross a few years after we did — pray with a mixture of the two approaches. I've found, for daily study each morning, that staying always with the same words is helpful to anchor and channel my thought. The words I use are these:

Beginning my study:

> Father, I come now to your word in Scripture, praying it would enter my mind that I know what You would have me do, my will that I am moved to do it, and my heart that I love the doing of it and hate any disobedience to it.
>
> This is my only true food. Please nourish me with it for today. I pray you would humble me to obey You and strengthen me to serve You — cleanse my sins, heal my hurts, shield me from harm. Arm and armor me to fight well today, Lord, as your soldier for the Cross of Christ, for the Church his body, and for his glorious kingdom that is to come.

Concluding my study:

> Father, thank you for feeding me with your Word. I pray it will burn in me like a fire and stir in me like a song, hour by hour today. I pray it will medicine me and nourish me in the way you know I need, by your will not mine.
>
> Let it repel me from doing wrong and impel me to do right. Protect me from the selfishness, temptation, and distraction that steal away your word.
>
> Keep me ever active in serving you by serving your people. In Christ's name, amen.

In my previous life as a student of Mary Baker Eddy, I always found it odd—yet charming—that she relates the story of a little Catholic girl who, upon losing her crucifix, exclaimed, "I have nothing left but Christ" (SH 238:9).

Our family has rejoiced to find that upon setting aside Mrs. Eddy's book and leaving her church, we have nothing left but Jesus and his book, the Bible. We have nothing left, that is, except everything.

Published in April 2010
on the Ananias website

HYMNS FOR HIM

How can impersonal Mind or Principle be "my best friend"? If heaven is the unchanging reign of Spirit or atmosphere of Soul, why do I need a Savior to "make my heaven secure"?

Members of Christian Science churches who stand up on a Sunday morning or Wednesday evening to sing the familiar Hymn 224, "O Lord, I would delight in thee," are hopelessly tangled in such contradictions as these—contradictions between Mrs. Eddy's metaphysics and the God of the Bible—whether they know it or not.

I and my family concluded we couldn't live without the intimate friendship of Father, Son, and Holy Ghost, "God in person," even if it meant a break with our Christian Science upbringing, a different way of reading the Bible, and a disorienting change of churches.

Did the faint echoes of the Gospel in this and many other "adapted" hymnal selections help move us to that conclusion? It's hard to say, but I believe Jesus uses every smallest opening to shine his saving light into the darkness of mankind's self-salvation fallacy.

Chisel-Marks

Take a moment and read below, the *Christian Science Hymnal* adaptation (1932) of John Ryland's original Baptist verses (1777). Where new phrasing has been substituted, Ryland's words are shown afterward in brackets.

Despite the metaphysical word changes — to avoid saying that the Creator made this earth, for example, or that Christ actually died — one senses line by line the insistent message of fallen man's need for a Savior who is, inconveniently, God in person!

Hymn 224: 'O Lord, I would delight in thee'
O Lord, I would [Grant Lord, I may] delight in thee,
And on thy care depend;
To thee in every trouble flee,
My best, my ever [only] Friend.
When all material [created] streams are dried,
Thy fulness is the same;
May I with this be satisfied,
And glory in thy name!

All good where'er it may [No good in creatures can]
be found,
Its source doth find [But all is found] in thee;
I must have all things [be blessed], and abound,
While God is [thou art] God to me.
O that I had a stronger faith
To look within the veil,
To credit what my Savior saith,
Whose word can never fail!

He that has [Thou that hast] made my [our] heaven
secure,
Will here all good provide;

While Christ is rich, can I [we] be poor?
What can I lack beside? [Christ who for us has died!]
O Lord, I cast my care on thee,
I triumph and adore;
Henceforth my great concern shall be
To love and please thee more.

Leafing through the *Christian Science Hymnal*, one finds in hymn after hymn as borrowed from other churches and modified to fit the Mary Baker Eddy teachings, the same chisel-marks of change and vestiges of gospel truth as we've just seen in No. 224.

In my final months before leaving the Christian Science branch church where I had earlier been First Reader, I would more often on Sunday mornings attend the nearly Anglican church where I was eventually to be baptized.

The hymns and prayers addressed to Jesus himself, our personal Savior, often brought me to tears. I was that starved for the warm presence of "God in person." Only much later did I realize that part of what had brought on that hunger and thirst, that tantalizing sense of something missing, was the hymnbook at my own branch church a mile away.

Published in April 2012
on the Ananias website

BROKEN CISTERNS

At our church on Christmas Eve, the sermon was on what St. Mark meant with his opening line about "the beginning of the gospel of Jesus Christ, the Son of God (1:1)"

At my son and daughters' church the previous day, the sermon was on what the angels meant by telling Mary, Joseph, and the shepherds, "Be not afraid" (Luke 2:10).

At every Christian Science church this past Sunday, by contrast, the lesson subject was "Is the universe, including man, evolved by atomic force?" That's the best Mrs. Eddy could do for loved ones of ours who attended those services in great need of the Christmas tidings of comfort and joy in Jesus' birth.

Thud. It was a jarring reminder of how Christian Science makes no provision for the climactic moments of the Christian year, our Lord's coming at this season or his crucifixion and resurrection at Easter. Though oddly it does bow to America's civic year with a special service on Thanksgiving Day.

Science and Health does mention the importance of hearing "the manger and the cross tell their story" (SH 142:15). But how vital can that story really be for Scientists who see the real man, Jesus included, as "never born and never dying" (SH 258:27 and 557:20)?

Thirsty

Eddy's comment that the story of the manger and the cross is wasted on a mentality of "pride and fustian" — that is, self-importance and pretension — has the sad irony of describing perfectly the intellectual inhumanity of her own metaphysics.

It was the detached, dismissive Christian Science attitude toward Christmas, explaining away the warm adoration of traditional carols and the miraculous nativity accounts in Matthew and Luke, that first began to propel my wife and me out of the Eddy orbit. We were thirsty for the living water of our Savior, Jesus the child of Mary, God incarnate. Mrs. Eddy gave us only dryness.

And this is the tragedy of Christian Science, as God warned long ago by his prophets: "My people have committed two evils. They have forsaken me the fountain of living waters, and hewed them out cisterns, broken cisterns, that can hold no water" (Jeremiah 2:13).

Father, Son, Spirit, thank you for the gracious, saving invitation in the closing words of the whole Bible, which I and my whole family have eagerly accepted, and which our pastor gave as the benediction the other day as we concluded Christmas Eve worship, "Let him that is athirst come, and whosoever will, let him take the water of life freely" (Revelation 22:17).

Published in December 2017
on the Ananias website

NOT REINVENTED

Lifting up "Jesus Christ, and him crucified," in the words of I Corinthians 2:2, is unusual for Christian Scientists. But word is getting around about a group in St. Louis who talk more like followers of the Cross than Mrs. Eddy's devotees usually do. What are we to make of them? What is going on? Are they reinventing church to recover the apostolic original?

Too many Scientists, objectively though not deliberately, come under Paul's awful verdict, "enemies of the cross" (Phil. 3:18) — in their case not owing to any materialism such as that verse suggests, but to a spiritual pride which in the end negates Jesus' atoning death just as fully and leaves the individual just as lost.

This group, though, calling themselves the Next Generation Christian Science Fellowship, claims to recognize the centrality of the Cross along with the gifts of the Holy Spirit and the ministry of evangelism.

These terms appear in a "covenant agreement" which members of the fellowship have signed. It was easy to find online — and copy — when the present article was written in 2009, but had

71

become unavailable on the Web by the time we were preparing for book publication in 2020.

It's not clear from a careful reading of that now-lost document, however, whether the members are struggling back toward the New Testament gospel or merely repackaging the Eddy teachings for contemporary tastes.

Do they feel the relentless pursuing love of the Hound of Heaven, as we who manage the Ananias website did in making our way from Boston to Calvary — or is this just word games, designer spirituality, packaging?

Closer to Calvary?

Ten questions presented themselves when I read the Next Generation Fellowship's covenant. They were submitted to Fellowship officers but never received a reply. The numbered questions appear below in regular type after each indented paragraph of the NGF document.

A curious mind may draw one closer to Calvary, perhaps even to the very hilltop. But only the surrendered heart can truly dwell there and find salvation in the wondrous Cross. Will this be the outcome for NGF Christian Scientists, whatever may have been their intent in first coming near? I pray it will.

> *Next Generation Christian Science Fellowship/*
> *Covenant Agreement*
>
> Encouraging growth in grace through worship, education, and service in a joyfully inclusive and loving community. These convictions bring us together as a faith community. We hold in common that: The purpose of life is to glorify God and joyfully to celebrate the defining, creative, and loving presence of God in everything we do.

Question 1. In "echoing the Westminster Confession," as a footnote says the above statement does, are you also accepting its definition of God in three Persons, Father, Son, and Holy Ghost?

The inspired Word, Logos, or Christ revealed in the Bible is our sufficient guide to eternal life. This includes embracing not just Jesus' teachings but the fullness of his life—which he said demonstrates the design of the Bible and God's intent for salvation, healing, and wholeness

Question 2. Does your concept of "our sufficient guide" allow the Bible to be its own key, or is *Science and Health* indispensable for correctly understanding God's Word? In "embracing the fullness of [Jesus'] life," do you accept that he was God incarnate, who died to save us from our sins? (I Cor. 15:3).

Following Christ in the way of God's choosing is the means by which Mary Baker Eddy repeatedly said Christian Science could be correctly understood and her teachings broadly shared with humanity. The school whose schoolmaster is not Christ, gets things wrong.

Question 3. Does your way of "following Christ" include worshiping Jesus as Savior and Lord? Does it include taking communion with bread and wine in remembrance of his body and blood?

Spiritual healing is a natural sign following the transformative power of the Spirit at work on one's character and the entirety of one's life and relationships. Physical healing alone is insufficient as the primary incentive for, or validation of, one's spiritual commitment.

Question 4. Do you accept that spiritual and physical healing can really occur through the prayers of any Christian, not just Christian Scientists?

The centrality of the cross, consistent with the teachings of Mary Baker Eddy, embodies the essential evangelism of the human ego, the necessity for the surrender of any source of meaning and purpose apart from God. In the cross the inseparability of divinity's embrace of humanity is made clear, and individuals feel God's love right where they are in their experience.

Question 5. When you relate the cross to "the inseparability of divinity's embrace of humanity," are you agreeing that each of us is a real sinner in need of a Savior, and that Jesus' real death was the necessary sacrificial atonement to meet that need?

Binding up the broken-hearted and demonstrating extraordinary love is reflective of the highest practice of Christian Science. In consonance with the Bible and Christian Science, the genuine expression of our humanity is the primary indication of what we understand of God.

Question 6. Does "your demonstrating extraordinary love" include welcoming into the fellowship those who use medicine, alcohol, or tobacco?

"Judge not that ye be not judged" and "let every person examine himself or herself" are the hallmarks of biblical and Christian faith, and of the practice of Christian Science. Great perversion of Christian faith occurs when people feel criticism and judgment of their worth in the midst of Christian community.

Question 7. Does your "judging not" result in acknowledging Catholic, Protestant, and Orthodox believers as no less true Christians than Mrs. Eddy's followers?

Love is the defining characteristic of primitive Christianity and must remain so in any reinstatement of it today. We strive to offer a witness of love so radical that the world may not understand it even while people are irresistibly drawn to it. Caring for the community involves inward nurture of those who are part of this fellowship and outward embrace of the larger community and world in which we live. Our ideals must be practiced in tangible expression as proof of our prayer for enriched affections.

Reaching Youth and Young Adults with a ministry and fellowship that draws them to want to be involved in worship and service, spiritual education and growth opportunities, enhanced relationships and community, is a primary commitment of this Fellowship.

Equipping "the saints" for ministry is core to the mission of the Christian church and we strive to recognize the gifts of ministry given by the Holy Spirit to each individual, offer to support their development in service to the mission of this Fellowship, and afford opportunities for these gifts to be shared.

Question 8. Is it imperfect human beings, ordinary people in the flesh, who are given these gifts by the Holy Spirit, or do the gifts reside with some other entity: immortals, the ideal man, God's perfect child?

Evangelism, sharing the good news of God's love, is central to the calling of every follower of Christ and fulfills Mary Baker Eddy's definition of her church as an evangelical order. This Fellowship devotes itself, individually and corporately, to making a witness to the world of the truths it espouses.

Question 9. Does your "evangelism, sharing the good news of God's love," involve leading individuals to the New Testament gospel — "believe on the Lord Jesus Christ and thou shalt be saved," Acts 16:31 — or instructing them in Mrs. Eddy's metaphysics?

In Conclusion, John Asks:

<u>Question 10.</u> My inquiry into the foundations of your faith can be summed up in this: If someone ignorant of Scripture were to ask you the same two questions Pilate asked, "What is truth?" (John 18:38) and "What shall I do then with Jesus which is called Christ?" (Matt. 27:22), how would you answer?

As stated above, no one from the Next Generation Christian Science Fellowship ever replied to my 2009 letter of inquiry based on the foregoing ten questions.

But based on what I was able to observe in attending a 2014 Sunday service of theirs, and later in reading the sermons delivered by their leadership team on different occasions up to the current year, 2020, one thing is clear:

NGF has continued attempting to have one foot in the Mary Baker Eddy teachings and the other in a liberal (very liberal) Protestant reading of Scripture.

In a word, theologically lukewarm — and as such, unpalatable to the Lord Jesus, of which we're warned in Revelation 3:16. The very fact that NGF, at some point in the past decade, was able to clothe itself in the garb of a regular branch of the Boston organization and thus to operate now as First Church of Christ, Scientist, Brentwood, Missouri, says much.

To me it says that while these earnest seekers may have sincerely hoped to reinvent the Eddy church as an authentic New Testament church, they have yet to really do so. Jesus isn't satisfied with half our loyalty, as he makes clear in Luke 9:57-62. He wants our all, our everything.

Published in November 2009
on the Ananias website

SUNSET FOR EDDYISM

Dave Petteys, a follower of Jesus since the 1990s and my colleague in hosting the Ananias website, recently jotted some thoughts about the deepening decline of Mary Baker Eddy's movement. I came back with my own reactions to each of his observations. Here's our dialogue:

Dave: Having been raised in the Christian Science church, it's sad in a way to watch it self-destruct. The 2019 reissue of Caroline Fraser's 1999 book about the movement, *God's Perfect Child*, brings so many memories and emotions flooding back.

John: Sad, yes, in terms of important experiences we both had and good people we've known who followed Christian Science. But also sadly welcome, in terms of this whole web of harmful falsehood that needs to pass from the scene — the sooner the better

DP: Even as a youngster, I witnessed the church do nothing for its young. Any time anyone would try to do something, the Monitor Youth Forum or youth groups at the church, the elderly would grouse "It's not in the Manual" and veto it.

JA: And I witnessed the same thing with my parents' effort to do youth ministry for Scientists through the Adventure Unlimited camps and chapters in the 1950s, '60s, '70s. They were coldly rebuffed by the Boston hierarchy. It typified the inhumane, loveless absolutism Christian Science teaches.

DP: Nor was there any organized body of instruction at the Sunday school to pass on to the next generation. It often seemed that teaching Sunday school was an onerous task assigned to the newer members as an initiation. It meant the least experienced Christian Scientists were the ones doing the teaching.

JA: Not always; I had some excellent Sunday school teachers. But the Christian Science denial mentality had no more compassion for the young than it did for the elderly, the sick, the sinning, or the infirm. As a kid, as a teen, there's this eagerness for the world in all its glory. Science dismisses it as merely a dream. "Here's a 600-page book on metaphysics, have at it."

DP: So now as the movement shrinks, members dying off and churches closing, the only remnant will be a cadre of Mother Church officials in Boston managing and living off the huge endowment they still own.

JA: And ditto at Principia in St. Louis and Elsah, where an administrator blurted to reporters, "We're richer than God — but running out of students." The school has consequently begun admitting students who aren't Christian Scientists at all.

DP: The Christian Science church says it was established to "restore primitive Christian healing." They go so far as to call Jesus "the first Christian Scientist." No, he was God incarnate whose atoning death saved the world, something CS denies. Here on earth, Jesus' mission was to bring "the Kingdom." His healings were only supportive and ancillary to that.

JA: He warns at the close of the Sermon on the Mount that at the judgment some will say they did mighty works in his name, but he will reply, "I never knew you." I think he's warning against spiritual pride that assumes self-salvation — Christian Science in a nutshell. He wants us meek, poor in spirit.

DP: We so often heard church members refer to "the pivotal healing," the Christian Science demonstration that brought them into the church. The downside is, of course, is that when a healing is not realized, then the faith is undone!

JA: Christian Science also talks as if there's no healing by prayer except with Mrs. Eddy's method, her supposed "Key to the Scriptures." Yet Christians all through centuries, Catholic and Protestant alike, have healed by prayer. The difference though, is that they see it as Jesus intended — one of the "things added" when you seek first God's kingdom and righteousness, sin forgiven, the new birth.

Wilderness Times

DP: The idea that a practitioner can conjure up the "healing power of Truth" and heal someone on command strikes me as heresy. It's magic, a manipulation of nature. I don't discount that there is faith healing. But it's done only in accordance with God's will, not the practitioner's. Example: if you were a practitioner in the Egypt of the Exodus, praying against the ten plagues, you'd be in trouble, wouldn't you? Something bigger was going on there — and is often going on in any illness.

JA: Suffering, struggle, sorrow, hardship, self-sacrifice, wilderness times, chastening — all have been part of God's gracious provision for his people's salvation and sanctification from Adam and Eve to John on Patmos to the martyrs of today. Christian Science completely misses that. It's a fraud on the believer and a false portrayal of what the human condition is about.

DP: Exactly, and thus another mistaken Christian Science article of faith is the "unreality of evil". Such a doctrine overthrows millennia of sacred history along with everyone's firsthand experience. To deny Satan exists is to allow him to have a field day with you. Then Mrs. Eddy oddly backtracks and talks about "malicious animal magnetism," which is an element of the spiritual warfare the Church has been fighting forever.

JA: Satan, evil, and our own sin nature cannot be wished away. Attempting to do is spiritual suicide. For me, this realization came after blowing up my marriage. The man I saw in the mirror wasn't "God's perfect child." He was reprehensible. For Katie Beim-Esche it was the horror of the 9/11 attacks. She went on to find Christ, and she now leads an important new ministry, the Fellowship of Former Christian Scientists. For some Eddy followers that turning point is the needless death of a beloved parent or child who was cruelly cut off from medical help.

DP: Tragic and avoidable. And then in Christian Science, there are no funerals. To die is to fail to realize your healing, and no one wants to talk about it. I can't tell you how many times it was "what happened to so and so? I haven't seen him for a while" "Oh you didn't hear? He died six months ago." So there is no sanctioned community support or comfort for loved ones left behind.

JA: Nor is there any accountability for the failures of the so-called "science" itself. Followers just go along telling each other that Christian Science heals, Christian Science works—except when it doesn't. A genuine science is objectively verifiable, consistent, yielding replicable results, and forthright when results don't match theory. Eddyism is none of those things.

DP: As the church members grow older, they continue to die off, to "fail to realize their healing" (as if all the members could live forever). The children of these older members see them refuse medical care and die sooner than they might have. Who knows? Would they have lived longer—a few months? A year or three?

He Found Us

JA: Many of these well-meaning Christian Scientists are mouthing words like "truth" and "love" yet acting out the opposite, heartlessness and delusion. Talking of "treatment" while in many cases treating nothing. So very sad.

DP: Not that conventional medicine and drugs, what Mrs. Eddy quaintly calls "Materia Medica," is always the answer either. Doctors of questionable ethics perform massively expensive medical procedures on very elderly patients, like a hip replacement on a 90-year old. You have to wonder if it is for the patient's benefit or a "cashectomy" for the provider, the system on autopilot.

JA: That, and the fact that some conditions are just beyond the knowledge or ability of medicine at its best, its most ethical and compassionate, to heal. There's a tragic dimension to life in this fallen world that the Eddy doctrine ignores, leading to so much heartache. No one is immune to selfishness and sin, not the MD, not the CSB. We can't perfect ourselves or save ourselves. We need Jesus for that. What a blessing that you and I found him. Or rather—he found us.

John concludes: Dave and I met in the 1970s as members of Sixth Church Denver, the largest Christian Science congregation in Colorado. I came to the Cross in the 1980s, he a decade later. Now that Dave is 81 and I'm 76, sunset is coming for us. After that, eternity with Jesus, the Light of the World. Sunset for Mary Baker

Eddy's movement is also coming. May it lead to countless Christian Scientists being reborn through Christ as we were.

Published in August 2019
on the Ananias website

Annunciation by the angel Gabriel to the Blessed Virgin (Dore)
Had I been looking to the wrong Mary all along?

CHAPTER 5:
WHY TAKE HER WORD
FOR IT?

As a child I was in awe of the radiant portrait of a white-haired lady in our Sunday School room. This, we learned, was Mary Baker Eddy, the Discoverer and Founder of Christian Science, our beloved Leader. Was our church odd for revering her that way? No, to us the oddity was in other churches displaying pictures of Jesus. Then at last I began to realize the strangeness of it all. Who was this Mrs. Eddy anyway?

SOMEONE TO REVERE?

"What shall I do then with Jesus who is called Christ?" asks Pilate in Matthew 27:22. I decided many years ago, after half a lifetime in Christian Science, that my own answer to that question must be to acclaim Jesus as Savior and Lord and thus to place him on the throne of my heart. After a period in the wilderness, this led to my leaving the Christian Science church and becoming a baptized Christian.

I did not, however, even then, decisively renounce Mary Baker Eddy or her book, the purported key to the Scriptures. That took still more time. And why? Perhaps hearing about my experience of the "in between" can help you in making a clean break, or in supporting other former Scientists as they do so. Or perhaps you will choose to try and remain in-between. I hope not. In any case, here is my story.

The liberating, indeed astounding, experience of daring to read the Bible on its own terms, instead of through the lens of Mrs. Eddy's writings, convinced me rather quickly that she had not given, as claimed, the "final revelation" of God's truth, man's identity, and Scripture's meaning (SH 107:5).

Far from being "God's perfect child," I realized the bad news that I was a sinner in need of a Savior—along with the good news that Jesus, God incarnate, had lived and died and risen for me personally, as exactly that Savior.

Though indeed a mystery, this was anything but a secret. I realized that he had again and again witnessed of himself in those very terms, as did the entirety of the Old and New Testaments, for anyone with eyes to see. Only my Christian Science blinders had concealed it from me.

No Friend, No Seer

Where then did this leave Mary Baker Eddy? It now dawned on me that she was obviously not the woman in the Apocalypse, foretold in Revelation 12. Nor was she the woman whose leaven transformed three measures of meal, seen in Matthew 13:33. Nor was hers the "little book" brought by an angel in Revelation 10.

And I readily saw that following her in everything, as devout Christian Scientists do, would be a mistake even in terms of her own repeated injunction to follow her "only so far as she follows Christ" (*Message for 1901*, 34:25, and *Message for 1902*, 4:4) — a standard which any fair-minded reader of *Science and Health* could recognize was, to put it mildly, not entirely met.

Yet I was so conditioned by four decades of hero worship toward her as "revered Leader, Discover and Founder," ingrained by the Christian Science culture, that I clung to the habit of following her at least in a degree.

Part of that, I see now, came from the Gnostic rush of in-crowd allegiance to Someone Special who had revealed to us, the favored few, Something Hidden and Exclusive. I have a painful reminder of this in an embarrassingly off-center statement of faith I wrote for a few friends in 1995, fully two years after my baptism.

There I loyally called *Science and Health* "a wise and strong friend to me" — though denying it is any sort of key to the Scriptures — and I favorably described Mrs. Eddy as someone I could still "treasure, despite our disagreements, among those holy seers through the centuries who have witnessed for Jesus in ways encouraging us to higher discipleship."

God help me, how brainwashed those words seem now. And yet how typical of the deep, earnest, unthinking hold the Eddy cult of personality — a blunt term, but let's call it that — has upon so many who have broken doctrinally with Science yet still cling sentimentally to its prophetess.

Soon enough I realized the perversity and peril of my remaining in-between in this way. I was in that dangerous position Paul warns against, of letting my "mind be corrupted" by someone "preaching another Jesus [and] another gospel" (II Cor. 11:4, repeated in Galatians 1:6).

Having decided I wanted the real Jesus, second Person of the Trinity, whose death on the cross bought me eternal life and pardon from sin, why on earth would I regard the book that denied or clouded these vital truths as a "friend," or its author as a "seer"? Why would I ever open it again, or encourage others to do? The blasphemy of it all, hit me like a thunderclap.

More Harm than Good

The question I posed earlier now came back to me with greater force and clarity: Where did this leave Mary Baker Eddy? Was she a gifted, well-intentioned, but spiritually confused eccentric? Or a charismatic, manipulative, glory-seeking charlatan? Or was she something worse — an unwitting or witting tool of the Enemy?

I honestly don't know, and I don't choose to speculate. What would be the point, after all? I've concluded, though, that Mrs. Eddy as Jesus would classify her is less like that scribe whose reverence for God placed him "not far from the Kingdom" (Mark 12:34) and, sad to say, more like those doers of wonderful works to whom the Lord says, "I never knew you" (Matthew 7:23).

Friends who have left Christian Science but still hold her in high regard will tell me she got a lot of things right in her writings and in her lifework. Maybe so, but for me as a Bible-believing Christian she got all the big things wrong: creation, sin, salvation, the Fall, the Cross, matter and spirit, time and eternity, heaven and hell. All of that and more. This woman, even if she meant no harm, has done more harm than good. This is no seer, no friend of mine. Sorry.

And consider this in closing: Mrs. Eddy was so breathtakingly confident and grandiose in the claims she made about herself and the predictions she made about her legacy. She asserted that before the year 2000, if her followers kept faith, "Christendom will be classified as Christian Scientists" (*Pulpit and Press*, 22:13).

Elsewhere she went further, adding no conditional "if," and predicted that "Christian Science is destined to become the one and the only religion and therapeutics on this planet" (*Miscellany* 266:32).

Really, is there any other word for this but hubris? Megalomania even? She disclaimed being another Christ, but did call her "discovery" the second coming of Christ, or alternatively—never being very precise as a Trinitarian—the promised Comforter. Are we then to consider her one of those false prophets of whom Jesus and Paul told us to beware? It's hard to conclude otherwise.

Sad Conclusion

C.S. Lewis famously pointed out that the astounding things Jesus said about himself foreclose the possibility of regarding him as just a great human teacher. "He has not left that open to us. He did not intend to" (*Mere Christianity*, end of Chapter II.4).

Our only options are to accept him as indeed the Son of God, or to reject him as dishonest if not deranged—what has been called the "Lord, liar, or lunatic trilemma." And I have arrived, with sadness, at much the same conclusion in making sense of who Mary Baker Eddy was.

Her system is incoherent, self-contradictory, and in the last analysis does not work. It in fact damages people. Her church and movement are not sweeping the world but fading away. A century and a half on from 1866, Mrs. Eddy's "put me to the test" bravado has resulted in her unequivocally failing the test.

The world-historical greatness she took to herself turns out to have been a delusion. More than that, it seems, she was just not an admirable person. Not a good person. Not someone to revere or to follow at all. Someone that any of us who love Jesus Christ should entirely wash our hands of. Sorry.

Published in March 2019
on the Ananias website

FULL OF HERSELF

Who did Mary Baker Eddy think she was? Who did she think Jesus was? What was the Trinity to her? What was the Bible's authority to her? What did she think was God's plan for our salvation and for the outcome of history?

The height of her self-importance and the distance of her departure from historic Christian teachings are evident in a dozen lines (quoted in full at the end of this essay) from page 70 of Mrs. Eddy's autobiography, *Retrospection and Introspection.*

- In this passage, as I read it, she first assigns herself a role in the divine order of things that is coequal with the roles of Jesus and Mary and irreplaceable by either of them.

- Then she claims that the second coming is "unquestionably" her system, Christian Science, and not the bodily return of Jesus as foretold by himself in Matthew 24:64 and by angels in Acts 1:11.

- Finally, she seems to say (the wording is cloudy yet emphatic, a trademark of hers) that the "scientific ultimate" of Jesus' identity is "forever…incorporeal." This makes us wonder how she would square this assertion with the warning of I John 4:3 that "every spirit that confesseth not that Jesus Christ is come in the flesh is not of God."

Squaring her assertions with Scripture did not greatly concern Mrs. Eddy, however, nor does wonderment about the matter seem to concern her followers today. This was illustrated by the chance remark that led me to the passage we're examining.

To Each a Niche

After a Christian Science friend said jokingly that he was confident of his "own niche in time and eternity," I looked up the passage. Having not seen it in the twenty years since I quit studying the Christian Science writings, I was startled by the string of remarkable statements just noted.

In thinking further about my friend's jocular remark, I was left with a couple of questions.

First, how can it be that a theologically momentous claim like this one is so much taken for granted by the Scientists that they remember it chiefly for the aside about niches — and not for the central and profound points at issue?

And second (which may answer the first question), is it possible that the "niche" declaration bespeaks an individualism — or even a solipsism — so radical that every Scientist is tempted to count his own view of things as equally valid with Mrs. Eddy's or Jesus's or the Bible's view of things?

If this is the case for Christian Science followers — and based on my own long years as one of them, I think it very well may be — each person implicitly feels he has permission to pick and choose any mix or modulation of doctrines from the Bible and Mrs. Eddy that happens to suit him.

So when she ranks herself in an odd trinity with Jesus and Mary, if that seems a bit much for someone like my friend, you don't confront it, you just shrug it off. We've then gone beyond the Reformation teaching of "the priesthood of all believers" and arrived at the priesthood of *all,* period.

Customized Theology

The result? Individually customized designer theology for everybody, and no worries, mate. You don't have to "believe" in anything beyond your own niche in time and eternity.

This mentality slides easily into New Age spirituality, agnostic positive thinking, or a jaded sense that all religion is subjective and relativistic — the tragic end point of so many lost souls who break with Christian Science and replace it with one of those make-shift belief systems, or with nothing at all.

But if you are reading this and have broken with Christian Science or are thinking of doing so, it means you have not gone down that easy, empty, wide road and have instead found the narrow way of life in Jesus Christ.

That's the way that my wife and I and our children have chosen to follow have found, by God's grace. We gratefully anticipate eternal joy in the many mansions awaiting us with the Father, Son, and Spirit, the true and only Trinity — and no other niche do we desire.

Here is the passage discussed above, from *Retrospection and Introspection* by Mary Baker Eddy, page 70:

> (L.14) No person can take the individual place of the Virgin Mary. No person can compass or fulfill the individual mission of Jesus of Nazareth. No person can take the place of the author of *Science and Health*, the Discoverer and Founder of Christian Science. Each individual must fill his own niche in time and eternity.
>
> (L.20) The second appearing of Jesus is, unquestionably, the spiritual advent of the advancing idea of God, as in Christian Science.
>
> (L.23) And the scientific ultimate of this God-idea must be, will be, forever individual, incorporeal, and infinite, even the reflection, "image and likeness," of the infinite God.

Published in May 2011
on the Ananias website

REVISING THE TRINITY

Trinitarian Christians pray in the name of the Father, Son, and Holy Spirit. Mary Baker Eddy's followers worship a different trinity, as I was reminded recently by a friend's article in the Christian Science periodicals.

Their God, though usually called "He," is identified as both Mother and Father, and is more often impersonally described as Principle, Mind, Soul, Spirit, Life, Truth, and Love. God's messenger of the only way to know Him, Scientists believe, is Mrs. Eddy. The Comforter provided by Him through her, as Scientists read in their textbook, is Christian Science itself.

There are two problems with this feminized, modernized, intellectualized, depersonalized trinity. It is neither true to the Bible nor mighty to save.

Christian Scientists vaguely cite what they claim is scriptural authority for their reinterpretation of who God is, while ignoring the plain and plentiful texts that identify the true and only Trinity: Father, Son, Spirit.

Worse, although Scientists believe their approach heals and harmonizes human experience, it does not really address the sin problem for time or for eternity. Our ultimate reconciliation with a holy God is accomplished only by His Son's incarnate life and atoning death.

And our present escape from the trap of involuntary disobedience and broken resolves (as diagnosed by Paul in Romans 7:14-25) is possible only through the indwelling Holy Spirit. No such escape is possible through the self-salvation approach of "knowing the truth."

It's true that *Science and Health* can be quoted to argue that Mrs. Eddy didn't entirely reject the second and third Persons of the Trinity as given in the New Testament and the historic Christian creeds.

In practice, however, on the evidence of oral testimonies in Christian Science churches and writings in the *Journal* or *Sentinel,* one finds that the Son and the Spirit are indeed replaced by the Discoverer and her discovery in Scientists' religious life—much to their spiritual impoverishment.

For the Bible is very clear about the dire consequences of derogating either God's beloved Son (I John 2:22, 23) or His Holy Spirit (Mark 3:29). What kind of "revered Leader" would lead her followers into such a fearful wasteland of error?

Published in March 2009
on the Ananias website

THERAPEUTICS OR SALVATION?

Will Jesus return? Christians expect him to, based on the Bible. Christian Scientists don't, based on Mary Baker Eddy's writings. Her own appearing and lifework, she indicates, fulfilled his promise of reappearing.

The consequences of believing that are profound. They bear upon who he was or was not; whether any of his promises can be relied on, or the Bible itself; what we can or cannot expect from him in time or eternity. I want to explore some of those consequences.

Studying in Luke the other day, I came to the divine commission pronounced by the old priest Zacharias upon his newborn son, who would become John the Baptist: "And thou, child, shalt be called the prophet of the Highest: for thou shalt go before the face of the Lord to prepare his ways; to give knowledge of salvation unto his people by the remission of their sins" (Luke 1: 76, 77).

Because I still read each morning from the same Bible my parents gave me when I was an earnest young Christian Scientist just out of college, there are many notations dating from my years of correlating Scripture with the Eddy teachings. Next to this passage was jotted a citation from her *Message to The Mother Church for 1902*, page 16.

Whispered

There we find Mrs. Eddy's account of how God had "whispered" to her the name *"Science and Health"* for the untitled book she had been working on, and how gratified she was when later seeing that identical phrase in John Wyclif's early translation of the New Testament into English, where it stands as his rendering of the Luke 1:77 words, "knowledge of salvation."

What are we to make of this? The thought is just dropped there, amidst a 20-page ramble of many other thoughts, and not worked out. But it suggests that as of 1902, the Leader of Christian Science was inclined to view her textbook as a sort of second coming of John the Baptist. If that were the case, *Science and Health* would be in the position of a modern-day forerunner to Jesus, not a rival or replacement or successor for him. Hmmm.

Muddled and misleading as the claimed equivalence of the Luke 1:77 rendering might be — and more about that in a moment — this would be less theologically audacious than Mrs. Eddy's broad hint a couple of years earlier (*Message to The Mother Church for 1900*, 6) that *Science and Health* might well be the second coming of Christ.

The reason? Because "some modern exegesis on the prophetic Scriptures cites 1875 as the year" of that occurrence — and "in that year the Christian Science textbook was first published."

This stupendous claim echoed a similar assertion she had made in 1891: "The second appearing of Jesus is, unquestionably, the spiritual advent of the advancing idea of God, as in Christian Science" (*Retrospection and Introspection*, 70).

And much the same identification of her work with the Lord's return appears at least twice within the pages of *Science and Health* itself. There she first reads Jesus' parable of leaven placed by a woman into three measures of meal as "foretelling the second appearing in the flesh of the Christ, Truth," and she proceeds to interpret those three measures as signifying science, theology, and medicine (SH 117:31).

Then later in the same chapter (which bears that very title, "Science, Theology, and Medicine"), she says that the widespread contemporary demonstration of "the healing power of Truth as an immanent, eternal Science" amounts to nothing less than "the coming anew of the gospel of 'on earth peace, good-will toward men'" (SH 150:6).

And to whom did that gospel in its first coming pertain? To no one other than Jesus Christ, of course — the Virgin's child and God's only begotten Son.

Substituted

It's true that in offering her "Key to the Scriptures," Mrs. Eddy did not directly reject or reinterpret the clear promises of Jesus' literal and physical second coming that are given with his own words in Matthew 26:64 and with the angel's words in Acts 1:11.

No, she simply ignored those texts and substituted her own semi-mystical insinuations (obliquely leading the reader, never quite blunt) about 1875 as the end times and herself with a central role therein. Quite extraordinary when you think about it, really.

Was it actually a cult to end all cults that she set out to establish, a system "undoubtedly...destined to become the one and the only religion and therapeutics on this planet" (*Miscellany*, 266:29), in which she would fulfill prophecy as the anointed revelator?

Or was she simply "a willing disciple at the heavenly gate" (SH ix:16), the founder and first among equals in an evangelically-inclined "church without creeds...which should reinstate primitive Christianity and its lost element of healing" (*Manual*, 17:3)?

I honestly don't think she herself knew which of these guiding visions was decisive with her from one day to the next. Charitably we can say it may indeed have been the second, more modest one.

But it is clear (or she would not written as she repeatedly did) that the more grandiose vision tempted Mrs. Eddy powerfully, and at last fatally. Satan desired (as the Lord warned Simon Peter, Luke

22:31) to have her and to sift her—and in this he was, I sadly conclude, all too successful.

But let me add this: If you are reading this and you are a Christian Scientist, an Eddy follower, the Adversary's success with her can be turned here and now into his failure and defeat with you. "Believe on the Lord Jesus Christ, and thou shalt be saved, and thy house" (Acts 16:9).

If you are reading this and you are a former Christian Scientist, now a follower of Jesus alone, join me in praying that the enemy's grip over this and this and this one, over all who wordlessly yearn to be saved, can be broken, stripped, swept away at this moment.

What Salvation Means

What do those words mean, after all: "to be saved"? Salvation is defined by Mrs. Eddy in the glossary of her textbook as, in part, Life understood and sickness destroyed (SH p. 593:20). On that basis one might plausibly equate the two phrases with which we began this discussion, "knowledge of salvation" thus becoming synonymous with "*Science and Health.*"

But what if, on the other hand, you and I as descendants of Adam and Eve are far too lost and bent and broken to ever straighten ourselves out by thinking better?

What if we're all sinners in need of a savior, and that savior was (still is, will always be) the one and only Lamb of God proclaimed by John the Baptist, the crucified and risen and soon-returning Jesus Christ, God incarnate from the Virgin's womb?

In that case, salvation means infinitely more than can even be remotely approximated by a "scientific system" for bodily health (SH 123:17). Wyclif's rendering of Luke 1:77 would be no more than a linguistic misstep, eventually set right by the King James translators, however much Mrs. Eddy may have wished it otherwise.

Then finally, to conclude, consider just how well the title she gave *Science and Health,* whether God-whispered or merely thought up, does in fact describe the book's main thrust and the main thrust of her movement for 150 years.

Do the book and its devotees seek to honor God and to live holy lives? Indeed so. But is not Christian Science *primarily* a quasi-scientific system for helping the individual realize bodily health (and overall wellbeing) by thinking better? Indeed so again. Undeniably so.

Try as she might to dress up that system as the Baptist's salvation-heralding message revived in America, the Bethlehem gospel come anew in Boston, Mrs. Eddy's followers then and now have always really measured its value in therapeutics. She specifically urged them to.

'But It Heals'

Think of the stopper you get without fail from a Christian Scientist when trying to show him or her who Jesus is and why the Cross matters and how *Science and Health* misrepresents those things: "But it heals," they insist; "it works." As if that settles the whole matter; and for them it does.

"Ye seek me," said Jesus to the crowds, "not because ye saw the miracles, but because ye did eat of the loaves, and were filled" (John 6:26). Scientists may say this does not apply to them at all, since Jesus' signs and "demonstrations" do interest them greatly; but I believe it applies with exactness.

To Mrs. Eddy and her followers, the miraculous signs are of interest only because they point to divine Principle and impersonal Science, not because they confirm Jesus as Lord of his own creation and personal Savior — the confirmation he cited to his cousin John (Matthew 11:4).

My Christian Scientist friends may feel wounded to have me suggest that their fidelity to the Eddy system results mainly from having "eaten of the loaves and been filled." No offense is meant. I am just trying to make sense of the way you believe and act. For it is the same way I once believed and acted.

It baffles and saddens me that when we who follow Jesus begin to reason with you who follow Mrs. Eddy, about the Lord's invitation to the great supper at which one can eat of his very flesh and blood and come into eternal life, your reply tends to be, "I have bought a piece of ground…have me excused" (Luke 14:18).

In other words, it seems you are so invested in something that yields earthly provision, that you don't care to join the Son of God for a heavenly feast.

"I stand at the door and knock," says Jesus in Revelation 3:20. "If any man hear my voice, and open the door, I will come in to him, and will sup with him, and he with me." Are you indifferent to his knock and his voice, I wonder, or don't you even hear them? Probably the latter.

Jesus offers you salvation, and we who follow him do our best to present that offer in language you can understand—but you speak another language that has defined salvation down to signify therapeutics and little more.

You follow a leader who has reworded Scripture into her own foreign tongue beyond anything Wyclif or Tyndale ever attempted. So even as we talk to each other with all the goodwill in the world—and goodwill you have in plenty, no one can doubt that—you and I only talk past each other. It's heartbreaking.

Published in July 2012
on the Ananias website

MBE'S PRIDE
OR JOB'S HUMILITY?

Life is unfair. Bad things happen to good people. Prayer may receive answers we can't make sense of. Suffering isn't always explicable. The world is broken.

To know all this, and still have faith that God loves us lavishly, is spiritual maturity. Not to know it is a formula for endless struggle with God and with ourselves. Christian Scientists tend not to know it—and pay the price.

It's the crucial lesson of the book of Job, dramatized more clearly there than anywhere else in the Bible, and Mary Baker Eddy utterly misses it.

After quoting in her textbook the opening of Job's final declaration to God, "I have heard of Thee by the hearing of the ear, but now mine eye seeth Thee" (42:5), she states cheerily that from this "higher standpoint, one rises spontaneously...attain[ing] bliss... and conquering all" (SH 262:17-26).

Wrong. Such triumphalism is the very opposite of Job's sorrowful confession concluding this passage, which she fails to quote. "I abhor myself," he admits contritely, "and repent in dust and ashes" (42:6).

When Mrs. Eddy claims that the correctness of her way of reading Scripture "may be seen by studying the book of Job" (SH 321:2), she's wrong again. A look at her two dozen citations to that book in *Science and Health* and *Prose Works* shows that she neither studied it herself nor can reliably guide the reader in doing so.

Rather she and her editors have merely mined Job for fragmentary proof texts they can twist to bolster her theories. A few examples:

- When Job laments in the depth of his undeserved, unfathomable travail, "The thing which I greatly feared is come upon me" (3:25), meaning only that he had worried the good times might be too good to last,

MBE uses the quote to imply that his fear was what had caused it all (SH 411:1).

That is, she blames the victim—exactly what Job's false comforters did, of whom God angrily said, "ye have not spoken of me the thing that was right" (42:7). And exactly what Christian Science has been doing for 150 years with its guilt-ridden theology of works righteousness.

- When Job defiantly insists, "Yet in my flesh shall I see God" (19:26), anticipating the resurrection of the just, based on his faith that "my redeemer lives, and that he shall stand at the latter day upon the earth" (19:25), MBE explains away the second quote (SH 320:31) and uses the first to argue that Job was expressing "assurance that the so-called sufferings of the flesh are unreal" (*Unity of Good* 55:17).

That is, she reads her Gnostic metaphysics back into this classic testament of suffering borne and surmounted, suffering never in the least negated—a testament that contains no hint of the Christian Science reality/unreality dualism anywhere in its 42 chapters.

Children of Pride

Mrs. Eddy claims in her autobiography (*Retrospection* 30-31) to have discovered through her own sufferings a "system" for relieving the sufferings of humanity with "the absolute proof and self-evident propositions of Truth," equating these with what Job 40:19 calls "the ways of God." Wrong yet again.

It's but another echo of the haughty intellect of the false comforters, who for all their wordy diatribes fail to see there is nothing systematic or self-evident about the deep mysteries of God and his purposes for us. Even his mighty beasts should serve to teach us of mystery, not of system, thunders the Almighty as he completes the humbling of Job in chapters 40 and 41.

So we find the Creator of the universe describing the fearsome behemoth as "the chief of the ways of God" in 40:19 (that text we just saw MBE rip from its context), and hailing the untamed leviathan as "king over all the children of pride" in 41:34.

It's not propositional truth, but the experiential wisdom of knowing how little one knows, that we see at work here. Job submits abjectly in his very next speech, confessing: "I uttered that I understood not, things too wonderful for me" (42:2).

"The greatest of all the men of the east" when we first meet him (1:3), Job at last comes to know himself one of those very children of pride—after losing everything and hitting bottom. We then see his repentant humility rewarded when "the Lord blessed the latter end of Job more than his beginning" (42:12).

Mary Baker Eddy, in contrast, never comes near admitting that she too is among the children of pride—never bows to any kingship higher than her own vaunted sense of self.

The Christian Science founder is too busy proof-texting and system-building to stop and face the profound questions of theodicy we encounter in Job's story:

Why did so much woe befall this "perfect and upright man" (1:8)? What was Satan up to? Why did God let him test Job? Where exactly are the comforters wrong? Why does the drama abruptly end without explicit answers? How does all this foreshadow the Cross?

MBE takes up none of these tragically, gloriously difficult issues. When you think about it, how could she? Their mystery would spoil the proud metaphysical mastery Science fraudulently promises its adherents.

System or Mystery?

Believing herself to be the instrument of revelation, she has no use for what was called by Jesus "the mystery of the kingdom" (Mark 4:11) or by Paul "the mystery of godliness" (I Timothy 3:16).

Alluding to the latter passage, she dismisses it as "the mystery always arising from ignorance of the laws of eternal and unerring Mind" (SH 145:20). Once more we hear an echo of Job's comforters with their smug certitudes. And what exactly was the battle-hardened Paul trying to spell out for young Timothy? Just this:

> "Great is the mystery of godliness: God was manifest in the flesh, justified in the Spirit, seen of angels, preached unto the Gentiles, believed on in the world, received up into heaven" (I Timothy 3:16).

Again it is easy to see why Mrs. Eddy would not want to grapple with, let alone submit to, any such proclamation of Jesus Christ as God Incarnate. Far too much humility is required.

She instead reinterprets Paul's words about God "manifest in the flesh" as a reference to "divine metaphysics," in the next breath after having reinterpreted Job's exclamation that "now mine eye seeth Thee" as a reference to "ever-operative divine Principle" (*Miscellany* 109:12-25). Everything must be made to fit into her system.

That there might be a reality of sheer grace transcending all systems, she cannot admit. "In vain," MBE remarks in her textbook, "do the manger and the cross tell their story to pride" (SH 142:15). And here she is right for once.

The story of the manger, a God who loves us enough to become a helpless, voiceless baby in a peasant girl's womb, and the story of the cross, a God who forgives us enough to bear away all our sins by dying a criminal's death, are lost on the would-be revelator with her lofty intellect, cold propositions, and seven synonyms for a distant impersonal God.

For some reason the Christian Science founder preferred a religion of diagrams and theorems to a religion of picture and story. As a result she lost out—and so have her followers, sadly—on the pearl of great price, the treasure of all treasures, the sweet savor of knowing Jesus Christ. In sending him to rescue us, God "exalted them of low degree" while "scatter[ing] the proud," as the Virgin Mary sang (Luke 1:51, 52).

On Their Own

How can Christian Scientists feel they got the better of that bargain? Unable to companion with humble Job in the certainty that "my redeemer lives...yet in my flesh I shall see God" (19:25, 26), they are out on their own, alone with their comfortless comforters and their synonyms and their metaphysical work as prescribed by proud MBE, wondering and worrying: "Have I made my demonstration?"

Of all her theological thefts from the unsuspecting, this robbery of the magnificent message of the book of Job has to be one of the cruelest.

If you're a Christian Scientist reading this, know that you no longer need to be out on your own, for the Father and the Son and the Spirit invite you home—into fellowship with the faithful Job and his reborn family, into the great cloud of witnesses (Hebrews 12:1) who have learned that, yes, bad things may happen to good people but, no, the answers to prayer never ultimately fail to make sense when we love unselfishly as Jesus loved (Job 42:10, John 13:34).

Published in September 2020
on the Ananias website

NO NATAL HOUR

What does Christmas mean to me? It means exactly those "tidings of joy to all people" that the angel told the shepherds in Luke 2:11.

But to Mary Baker Eddy, based on her well-known article by almost that very title (*Miscellany*, 261), it meant something quite different. The sharp divergence had a lot to do with my leaving Christian Science for biblical Christianity.

"Unto you is born this day in the city of David a savior, which is Christ the Lord," says the angel. A human baby, Jesus by name and Christ by title, arrives at a specific earthly time and place and for a specific divine purpose: our salvation. Christmas means just that to me. On what higher authority should I believe it means anything else?

Mrs. Eddy, however, claiming higher authority, pointedly denies the proclamation of Luke 2:11. "Christ was not born of the flesh...of matter...of a woman," she writes in "What Christmas Means to Me." Indeed, Christ was "never born" at all. According to the Christian Science founder, Christmas merely "commemorates the birth of a human, material, mortal babe," period.

So much for another favorite Scripture, Matthew's statement that the virgin's son would be called, in fulfillment of prophecy, "Emmanuel...God with us" (1:23). At a dark time when I was feeling distant from God and defeated by my imperfections, this incarnational Jesus with his saving grace seemed like a lifeline to me.

I felt that Mrs. Eddy, in claiming he was nothing of the kind, was personally affronting me in a manner that was not only uncaring but unfair and untrue. The issue of Christmas, together with the issue of Easter, brought me to a choice between him and her. I chose him, and I have never been sorry.

Filtered Out

Singing all the traditional carols during my forty years as a Christian Scientist, I somehow filtered out the plain biblical meaning in line after line. Only after coming to the Cross did I see what had been there all along.

"Christ is born of Mary," it says in *O Little Town of Bethlehem*. But was he? Not in Christian Science belief, which thus voided the plea and hope of a later verse: "O holy Child of Bethlehem, descend to us, we pray. Cast out our sin, and enter in: be born in us today."

Why close ourselves off and exclude ourselves from that beautiful and transformative coming of Jesus Christ? It's up to each person, but my decision was to stop doing so. What a difference it has made in my life ever since.

Christian Scientists, of course have their own hymn or carol for the nativity-that-wasn't. It is Mrs. Eddy's poem "Christmas Morn" (*Christian Science Hymnal*, No. 23), which they understand to be theologically correct in a way that the old, sentimental songs of the season are not.

In addition to devaluing the Bethlehem babe exactly as the previously discussed article does, the poem includes this prayer: "Dear Christ…no cradle song, no natal hour and mother's tear to thee belong… Fill us today with all thou art, be thou our saint, our stay, alway."

I don't know about you, but between the messes I've made in my life and the some of the foulness I can see in my own heart, I need more than a saint or a stay. I need a Savior, the Son of God incarnate, born in the flesh to share my humanness, crucified for my sins, risen and ascended to the right hand of the Father where he intercedes for me even now.

Christmas according to Matthew and Luke offers me that Savior, Christ the Lord, God with us, heralded by a blazing star and an angel choir. Whereas Christmas according to Mary Baker Eddy obscures the Savior, diminishes him, dismisses him.

The question is inescapable for each of us. What does Christmas mean to you?

Published in December 2007
on the Ananias website

SISTERHOOD ASCENDANT

One spring day in 2020, I took a deep breath, opened my laptop, and at the risk of bruising some feelings, tapped out a few lines for the comments page of a major national website where Mary Baker Eddy's legacy had recently been honored in connection with Women's History Month. Here is what I wrote:

"I was raised in a family and community that revered Mrs. Eddy. I loved them and still do. But considered in the light of day, regrettably hers is not a legacy of honor.

"She undermined the Bible, the book that has done more for human flourishing than anything ever written. She diminished Jesus, the central figure of world history, in order to elevate herself and her own mystic theories.

"She encouraged a personality cult bathing her in semi-divine adulation—thereby ensnaring countless women and men in a psychological dependency that is the opposite of standing on one's own feet in a supposed 'time for thinkers' which she disingenuously proclaimed (SH vii:13).

"With grandiosity she predicted her system would take over Christianity by 2000 and the entire world of religion and health soon thereafter. Fortunately the opposite has occurred: Christian Science is quickly passing from the scene, after having deceived millions over the past 150 years, and with unnecessary suffering visited upon many of them.

"If your series for Women's History Month intends to honor contributions of genuine merit, not merely defiant gestures by self-seekers, Mary Baker Eddy does not qualify."

The article to which I was objecting had been published online by *Real Clear Politics* on March 16, 2020, entitled "Mary Baker Eddy: Christian Scientist and Persister." It was part of a Women's History Month series recognizing notable speeches by women, in this case Mrs. Eddy's address in Boston's Tremont Temple on March 16, 1885 (see *Miscellaneous Writings*, 95).

The writer, Dana Rubin, apparently not a Christian Scientist herself, approached her subject from today's prevalent assumptions of intellectual relativism (everyone has their own truth) and cultural Marxism (ideas gain validity from who says them, not from their correspondence to objective reality).

In a word, identity politics. The implication — not spelled out in so many words — was that Mrs. Eddy's speech on that occasion had merit because of how many chromosomes she had, and because she defied the "establishment," and because her church took a growth spurt after the Tremont address.

All that and the glorification of Mrs. Eddy simply for having been a "persister" against opposition. The latter has been a slogan of the feminist movement in recent years, with a wordplay on "sister" no doubt implied as well.

Valorizing Eve

Thinking back, I can remember the talking point of Robert Peel and other Christian Science apologists that Eddy's system deserved special admiration by virtue of her being female — an argument rooted in her own slanted scriptural interpretations beginning with Eve in Genesis (SH 533:26) and continuing all the way to the woman in Revelation 12 (SH 562:3).

Over against which, we who believe in the Bible as truly inspired and believe in truth as truly true (to use Francis Schaeffer's deliberately repetitive term) must adamantly resist that whole solipsistic, self-indulgent mode of thought, whether it comes from a devout Christian Scientist like Peel or a feminist ideologue like Dana Rubin.

Christian Scientists like to think that reality is spiritual not material, and that they live in the truth that makes free. But consider the slavish materialistic determinism implied in even suggesting to someone that *Science and Health* is the book to live by because you and the author have (at long last, after eons of male domination) the same number of chromosomes.

Read a person's DNA and make them your life-example accordingly? No, thank you. What happened to "there is neither male nor female, for you are all one in Christ Jesus" (Galatians 3:28)?

It's true that no such simplistic motivation as I have just described actually determines most Christian Science women's adherence to the Eddy system. But the very hint of such motivation by herself and her followers should shock us. What a fraud on women and men alike. What an insult to those "thinkers" whose day is claimed to have finally dawned in 1866.

Bottom line, this shallow and faddish little article by Ms. Rubin is one more reminder that the exaltation of subjectivity and selfhood so dominant — and so damaging — in our times was first a source of, and then a beneficiary of, the rise of Christian Science in the 19th and 20th centuries. The anti-human consequences have been extensive, as I pointed out in my online rebuttal.

For this and many other reasons, we must regretfully conclude that Mary Baker Eddy did not leave a legacy of honor.

Published in March 2020
on the Ananias website

ISN'T IT TRAGIC

"Would ye ascend the mountain…and drink from its living fountains?" So asks the mysterious Stranger to a group of laborers in the valley at the beginning of Mary Baker Eddy's brief, biblically resonant tale entitled "An Allegory."

Recently I met a Christian Science couple who have organized — and named — their successful international consulting business around this worthy goal of helping mankind up the hill. Admirable people, inspiring to talk with.

So after talking with them, I read through "An Allegory" (*Miscellaneous Writings*, 323) for the first time in many years — having discontinued my study of Mrs. Eddy's writings upon leaving the church in 1992.

Scripture citations in the text were marginally noted in my own hand from some long-ago study I had made of the piece. But something was glaringly obvious to me now which I had only half-sensed back then, on my way out of Science — the complete absence of the crucified and risen Savior from this story.

Mrs. Eddy does quote or paraphrase Jesus' words throughout the piece. She does explain near the end that "the mountain is heaven-crowned Christianity, and the Stranger the ever-present Christ, the spiritual idea which [acts to] acquaint sensual mortals with the mystery of godliness — unchanging, unquenchable Love."

But the man Jesus is never mentioned, his crucifixion and resurrection hardly hinted at. All the theology here implies self-salvation by thought and effort, not the rescue of lost humanity by the sacrifice and victory of the Son of God incarnate.

Next to her line about "mystery of godliness," for example, I had jotted I Timothy 3:16. Mrs. Eddy simply equates that mystery with Love, one of her familiar synonyms for Deity. But the Bible context, from which she has torn this rich phrase, spells out the mystery this way: "God was manifest in the flesh, justified in the Spirit, seen of angels, preached unto the Gentiles, believed on in the world, received up into glory." What a contrast.

Hill of Christian Science

The hill in this allegory is certainly not Calvary. We read nothing here of what an old hymn calls "the wondrous Cross on which the Prince of Glory died." The only cross spoken of, at the very end of the article, is that which a "follow[er] [of] the Way-shower," if he loves God and neighbor as commanded, will "safely bear...up to the throne."

There in her closing paragraph she tells us that fitness to "ascend the hill of Christian Science" is a matter of personal righteousness, much like the qualifications in Psalm 24 to go up the hill of the Lord. The whole thing has an Old Testament feel of heaven earned by law, devoid of New Testament gospel and grace.

Missing entirely is the good news from Hebrews 12:18-24 that "ye are not come unto the mount that might be touched, and that burned with fire…but ye are come unto mount Sion, and…the heavenly Jerusalem…and to Jesus the mediator of the new covenant."

Reading Mrs. Eddy's allegory of the Stranger, "Mr. Spiritual Idea" as she calls him, atop "the summit of bliss survey[ing] the vale of the flesh," I felt very sad for my new friends with the consulting business, sad for all Mrs. Eddy's followers.

Denying themselves access to the freely offered mystery of godliness, metaphysically insisting that God was *not* manifest in the flesh, they needlessly struggle to do so much with so little, trudging up an incline which — did they but know it — our gracious Lord has already climbed for us.

"If Christ be not risen," wrote Paul, "then is our preaching vain, and your faith is also vain" (I Corinthians 15:14). This is the tragedy of the Christian Scientists. They do admit the resurrection of the human Jesus, but their Christ is someone or something different, an abstraction called unchanging Love — not the God-man who redeemed us with his blood, the Savior of Romans 10:6-9 and the Apostles' Creed.[19]

Lacking the transforming help of the true, biblical Jesus Christ, the Scientist is left to think or will his own way out of the fallen Adam nature into the restored image of God, a discouraging and ultimately impossible task.

[19] See full text in Appendix B

Sonship for us sinners cannot be self-asserted. It can only be attained by adoption, and this requires a sponsor who has paid the price for us: the crucified and risen Christ. "If Christ be not risen," Mrs. Eddy's preaching, metaphysics, allegories, and scriptural keys are all in vain, as is her followers' earnest faith in all that. Isn't it tragic.

Published in November 2007
on the Ananias website

Jesus receives a night visit from Nicodemus

CHAPTER 6:
ARE YOU REALLY SEEKING TRUTH?

We're told the Christian Science textbook is dedicated to "honest seekers for truth."[20] If that in fact describes Christian Scientists, one should be able to reason with them about what truth is and how to find it. Here are some attempts I have made in that direction — or imagined making.

20 SH xii:26

IMPOSSIBLE STRADDLE

"Rabbi, we know that thou art a teacher come from God," says the night visitor to Jesus in John 3:2. This ruler of the Jews, Nicodemus, clearly feels drawn to the man of Galilee and has gone out of his comfort zone to learn more.

Yet when Jesus begins to teach him, the Pharisee pushes back, objecting as if to say, "Yes, but," or "Not really?" He's not ready to go all the way, to take the step from knowing *about* Jesus to *knowing* Jesus. The interview ends and we lose sight of Nicodemus for a long time.

I thought of their encounter when a friend of mine, Art, told me about the efforts he and some other Christian Scientists are making to follow both the Jesus of the Bible and the Mary Baker Eddy of *Science and Health*.

I struggled for twelve years to live and think that way. Finally I realized I had to choose, and my unreserved choice with a flood of joy and relief was Jesus Christ.

I can see now that during all that time I was in the position of Nicodemus, trying to temporize and theorize with Jesus. Or the position of the Judaizers in Acts 15:1, the Laodiceans in Revelation 3:16.

Straddling, mixing, bargaining, wanting Christ but on my terms. What I learned was, it doesn't work. It gains you nothing and costs you the pearl of great price. It puts off the new birth, to only your own detriment. It's folly.

I want to tell Art and his fellow seekers: Don't do it. Don't try it. Don't come all the way to his door and then only put one foot inside. Don't you see, brothers and sisters?

You can't temporize with Jesus.

You can't theorize with Jesus.

You can't negotiate with Jesus.

You can't bargain with Jesus.

You can't debate with Jesus.

You can't compromise with Jesus.

You can't improve on Jesus.

You can't combine Jesus with anything.

You can't yoke Jesus with anyone.

You can't dabble in Jesus.

You can't reinterpret Jesus.

You can't domesticate Jesus.

You can't update Jesus.

You can't edit Jesus.

You can't nibble on Jesus.

You can't advance beyond Jesus.

You can't cherry-pick Jesus.

You can't use Jesus.

You can't take half of Jesus.

You can't tell Jesus you love him "but."

You can't have "Jesus and."

All you can do with Jesus is either surrender to him, or not. All you can do is accept who he is, and be who he invites you to be, and do what he tells you: "Follow me, and let the dead bury their dead" (Matthew 8:22). Because to try and do anything less with him is to do nothing at all.

Nicodemus Returns

It is at a burial, in fact—Jesus' own burial—that we ultimately meet Nicodemus as a convert in John 19:39. He is done keeping his distance; no more theorizing and temporizing. He shows up with Joseph of Arimathea on the evening of Good Friday to do what little they can, tenderly, reverently, courageously, humbly, for the bloody and broken body of our Lord.

Enough of "knowing thou art a teacher come from God." This Nicodemus is a doer, no longer just a knower. His fully surrendered presence in this second night visit anticipates the words of surrender from another Pharisee turned Christian, St. Paul, who declared himself "determined *not* to know anything save Jesus Christ, and him crucified" (I Cor. 2:2).

During my Nicodemus years I remember straining to convince myself that when Mrs. Eddy quoted that great passage about Christ crucified, approvingly in her chapter on atonement in the textbook (SH 39:7), she meant it, and when she quoted it in her chapter on physiology (SH 200:25) for the purpose of contradicting and improving on Paul's words, she didn't mean it.

What a struggle that was. The intellectual gyration of holding two opposites in mind became spiritually exhausting, and I at last decided my only course was to surrender to Jesus whether or not Mrs. Eddy was ever going to.

I realized that even as much as she praised "the women at the cross" (SH 49:1), the mixed message of her writings left heavy doubt that she would have been there with them on that dark afternoon.

So how could I continue trying to follow this leader, if her path led elsewhere than to Calvary? It was with a sense of sadness and loss, but also a sense of relief at parting company with something unfruitful, that these conclusions settled in on me.

Problematic

Art, my friend who speaks for what he calls "the Christian Christian Scientists," points out that it is difficult to know what a writer thought or felt behind her actual statements on the page, and that in fairness to Mrs. Eddy one might regard her as having been "a work in progress" with deeper theological depths than may appear in the writings up to her death in 1910.

But even supposing we grant that, I repeat my question above: What kind of leader does this make her? What kind of revelator? Why remain entangled with her problematic legacy of "Jesus and"? For what possible gain or reward or nourishment or loyalty?

Art says it grieves him to keep hearing from Scientists that Mrs. Eddy's atonement chapter in *Science and Health* is the hardest one for them to relate to. But wouldn't it naturally be so, given the countless points of cognitive dissonance between that chapter and the rest of the book?

Just take the example I gave, where she exegetes I Cor. 2:2 in glaringly opposite terms on page 39 and page 200. This is the most confused kind of Nicodemus-style straddling. No wonder her followers sometimes lose track of who or what they are following. She lost track herself!

How grateful I am that after more than a decade in the spiritual nighttime, the theological in-between, I stopped being the Nicodemus of John 3 and became the Nicodemus of John 19. Which one are you?

Published in May 2013
on the Ananias website

FAMILY ISN'T GOD

Are family reasons keeping you in Christian Science? Most of us feel a natural reverence for "the faith of our fathers." But what is this really about? Although honoring our parents according to the Fifth Commandment is never optional, family loyalty is not a sufficient reason for accepting a particular belief about God.

Whereas a true faith is to any person's credit, no one's personal endorsement — whoever he is — can make something true. God is no respecter of persons, nor should we be.

St. Paul told the Galatians (1:13-16) that being "exceedingly zealous of the traditions of my fathers" was his mistaken reason for persecuting the Christians. All that changed when he realized that God had "called me by his grace" for a different allegiance and purpose.

Human ancestry was then overruled, said Paul, by the heavenly Father "who separated me from my mother's womb...to reveal his Son in me, that I might preach him among the heathen."

On trial before the Roman governor Felix (Acts 24:10-21), Paul said bluntly: "This I confess unto thee, that after the way which they call heresy, so worship I the God of my fathers." In other words, he is declaring that his Lord is now Jesus, who had called himself the Way, and whose followers named their religion by that same word.

Yet he still asserts the new religion's continuity with Israel's ancient faith. For in this speech Paul goes on to describe himself as "believing all things which are written in the law and in the prophets: and hav[ing] hope toward God...that there shall be a resurrection of the dead."

Contradictions

These are the only two places in the New Testament where the idea we commonly call "faith of our fathers" is specifically mentioned. Each passage only half-endorses the idea. Interestingly, Mary Baker Eddy associates herself with both of them. But she contradicts Paul's theology in doing so.

In her address at Tremont Temple in 1885 (*Miscellaneous Writings*, 96), replying to one of Boston's leading clergymen who had charged her with teaching "a creed of pantheism and blasphemy," she paraphrased Acts 24 with insistence that "after the manner of my fathers, so worship I God."

Her remarks on this occasion described God, Christ, and man in terms which the Bible doesn't contemplate and which 1800 years of believers didn't profess, however. So the bow toward tradition here seems more of a cover than a genuine confession.

Was Mrs. Eddy, in her own estimation and in the eyes of her students, Jesus' servant — or was she his successor? Mrs. Eddy's biographer Robert Peel, relating the Tremont episode in the second volume of his trilogy, pages 155-156, notes that the *Christian Science*

Journal's writeup of the affair called her "the faithful messenger of the Second Coming."

Peel also surmises that she must have felt as the Lord himself did, according to John 1:11 — "He came unto his own, and his own received him not." Oh really? Blasphemy indeed, might well have been the reaction of her accuser, Rev. Joseph Cook.

Mrs. Eddy's departure from inherited faith is also clear when Galatians 1:14 is truncated in the chapter on "Recapitulation," her classbook, so as to omit Paul's reference to the revealing and preaching of the Son: "But when it pleased God, who separated me from my mother's womb, and called me by His grace...I conferred not with flesh and blood" (SH 478:27).

Here again, as she so often does, Mrs. Eddy cites the Bible in a manner where ostensible agreement veils her distortion of its plain intent.

Who Hinders You?

Paul saw himself as honoring the old Jewish beliefs yet venturing beyond them at the impulsion of his personal encounter with Jesus, the prophesied Messiah. Mrs. Eddy claimed to honor the old Christian beliefs even as she dethroned Jesus from the supreme position Paul assigned him.

I love and honor my Christian Scientist forebears, but I must part with them in declining to embrace the Eddy doctrines — because I love my Lord and Savior more. As Jesus warns in Luke 14:26, "If any man come to me, and hate not his father and mother...and his own life also, he cannot be my disciple."

Never since Abraham has been it been enough for the people of God to simply worship as our parents and grandparents did, period. He expects each of us as individuals to hear Him, walk humbly with Him, and be holy as He is. He makes no exceptions. (See Deut. 6:4, Micah 6:2, and Lev. 19:2.)

In coming out of Christian Science, not without fear and trembling, we of the Ananias circle have had to take seriously Jesus' warning not to put family ties ahead of *Him*. To you as a Christian

Scientist now, we put the question Paul finally asked his Galatian friends (5:7): "Who did hinder you that you should not obey the truth?"

Published in March 2009
on the Ananias website

BEST DAY OF MY LIFE

Does your experience growing up as a Christian Scientist, or the experience of someone you know, match mine? I was raised to be a follower of Mary Baker Eddy, while also, in a lesser way, an admirer of Jesus as the most godlike of all Bible figures. Her picture hung in our Sunday School, his did not.

In adulthood, as a result of struggles and searching, my view of them changed. I began to regard myself as a follower of Mrs. Eddy and Jesus together — but putting her first.

Then while serving as a branch church reader, I came to a crisis of faith, endured a painful confrontation with fellow members, and redefined my allegiance yet again — now I was a follower of Jesus and Mrs. Eddy together — but putting her second.

Henceforth I would interpret *Science and Health* in terms of the Bible, rather than vice versa as before. That was a big step. It cast everything into a new and beneficially disturbing perspective.

But not until after another dozen years of wilderness wandering did I realize that each of us must choose — and choose decisively. We can either follow Jesus and his book, or Mrs. Eddy and her book. But we cannot follow both, since she contradicts him in fundamental and irreconcilable ways.

New Birth

Scripture teaches me that (1) Jesus was and is God incarnate, (2) I am a sinner in need of a savior, and (3) Jesus died on the cross to accomplish and finish my salvation.

Yet the "Key to the Scriptures" on which I was raised would have us believe none of those propositions is true. Rather Jesus was only a man, I'm sinless and perfect, his was but a "seeming death" (SH 45:11), and salvation is up to us, ours to achieve through understanding.

The best day of my life, indeed the first day of my new birth, was the day I quit trying to have it both ways, ceased following Mrs. Eddy or studying her book or attending her church, and received Christian baptism in order that I might eat of the body and blood of our Lord at holy communion — in order that I might belong to Jesus entirely and only.

To relate all this takes a few moments. To live through it and find my way at last, took decades. And it was hard! The confusion was intense. The wishful thinking was strong. The personal and emotional ties were powerful.

But what beauty, what joy, what freedom, what deep rightness, came with the final decision. What a sense of homecoming.

If you know anyone who is stuck in the middle as I was, why not send a copy of this article to that dear person and encourage him or her to contact me? I would love to have a conversation about this inescapable choice we each must make.

Published in August 2010
on the Ananias website

DESIGNER SPIRITUALITY DEFRAUDS

The widespread assumption that true goodness is achievable in human beings by one's own effort was vividly illustrated by recent exchange on social media. It started when I cited a half-joking remark by Mark Twain about the darkness within every human heart.

Though I went on to make no doctrinal argument, my passing reference to God was enough to start a reader named Diana (not personally known to me) fuming with wounded self-regard.

Another reader whom I don't know either, Dale, answered Diana cogently from a Christian point of view. When she resumed the debate a short time later, still mixing confusion and indignation, it now seemed Diana was embracing the very God she had disavowed earlier.

This kind of "designer spirituality" too easily entraps many well-meaning individuals — including numerous former Christian Scientists who have shrugged off biblical religion in favor of making up a faith of their own.

Diana, quoted below, doesn't seem to have a Christian Science background. Yet her self-invented beliefs as expressed here could easily come out of the mouth of a fallen-away Mrs. Eddy follower. And it's all a cheat. It doesn't nourish. It's not the answer.

Looking ahead, though, the fraudulent solipsism of designer spirituality such as this woman espouses could become the dominant American worldview in our times — if Bible-believing followers of Jesus Christ don't pick up their game.

Village Square

This all happened among three complete strangers who encountered each other on Facebook, the village square of the 21st century. Here's how it went:

John: Mark Twain said we all have a moral sense that tells us what is good and how to avoid it, and an *immoral* sense that tells us what is bad and how to enjoy it. Wickedly cynical, and not the last word about mankind biblically.

But looking around us (and into our own hearts), it seems all too true. Hence to the question, "Can we be good without God?" — my answer is no.

Diana: I respectfully couldn't disagree more, John. I'm a good person, mother, friend, etc., I do many good deeds, I am spiritual, but I have no relationship with God (with a capital G). Being good is in the fabric of who I am, it doesn't come from reading the Bible or having a priest (especially one who rapes children) tell me what to believe.

I am a better Christian than many Christians who are so in name only. Religion relieves people of personal responsibility — it just says sin and repent and all will be well. Your question makes my point. I believe in not committing the sin in the first place. And defining "sin," that's a whole other story. To tell a child he or she was born of sin has been a tragic disservice to humankind.

Dale: I understand what you are saying, Diana, and there is certainly a great deal of validity, in the fact that you recognize moral right and wrong without having a relationship with God. You're also correct in claiming that just professing Christianity does not by itself make one good, or any better than the non-believer.

It's common today for everyone to think of themselves as a good person, according to their own definition of what good means. But unfortunately, by the standard definitions, and God's definitions, it's not like that. God has defined what is good, and no matter what any of us say or do, that will not change.

As a Christian, I will have to give an account of every sin I commit, whether I knew it was sin or not, whether I meant to hurt anyone or not. I do not claim any betterness relative to the next person, let alone any perfection, since I know I am just as sinful as they are. So being a Christian does not negate my sinfulness. But because I have recognized that I *can't* be good enough to earn my own salvation and then accepted God's gift of forgiveness, I will not have to pay the penalty.

He Sends Us Jesus

Of course that does not give me a license to keep on sinning, I am expected to do my best to change my behavior. Much false religion does tend, as you said, to "relieve people of responsibility" But true religion does not. The Bible does not. It holds us all accountable. That may not be obvious to you or even to some professed Christians, but in the end it will be.

As for your reference to the doctrine of original sin, a lot of misunderstanding surrounds that. It is certainly not meant to engender morbidity or self-disgust in children. Of course not. The relevant Bible passages just teach with complete realism that we all tend toward sin from our earliest beginnings, that we can't rescue ourselves from it without God's help, and that he sends us that help in the person of Jesus crucified and risen. Plus the challenge, in light of all that, for each of us to change our behavior, striving be more like God.

Diana: I appreciate your comments, but I have no use for another human being interpreting God for me. It is sacrilegious for any human being to think they understand God and can interpret God.

My relationship with God is between me and God. I do not believe we are separate from God. The dualism foisted on the human race by religion is what led us out of the Garden of Eden.

I live my life by the supposed Ten Commandments, but not because I read the Bible. It's just common sense to me. [End of Facebook exchange]

Facing the Sin Problem

"Just common sense," she says. My heart goes out to Diana and the millions like her in America today who are trying to navigate by impulse and improvisation through all the timeless moral and spiritual concerns of human history.

In the opening round she breezily claims to have no relationship with God. In the closing round she defensively admits to having one, but bristles that the details are nobody else's business.

And so it goes. She tosses around a term like "sacrilegious," untroubled by the lack of any agreed meaning or binding effect for sacrilege in the religionless or religion-defying world she seems to inhabit.

She's proud of upholding—by sheer intuition, it would seem—the "supposed" Ten Commandments. Even the first four of them, which prescribe our duties toward God, one wants to ask her?

Dale, her interlocutor in this odd back-and-forth, might not be quite the star of his catechism class, not quite ace his theology exam. But bravo to Dale for at least taking the Bible seriously, facing up to mankind's sin problem, and charitably engaging the poorly-informed in a chatroom as we've watched him do.

Why, you ask, have I bothered to transcribe their little chat for this collection of essays on coming to know the true and living God? Because the closer one looks at the Mary Baker Eddy's textbook and its manifold contradictions to the Bible, the more you start to see that Christian Science itself is but one more instance of designer spirituality, albeit elaborately developed and fancily dressed.

And why does that matter? Because at the end of the day, designer spirituality defrauds. Always has, always will. Self-salvation simply doesn't save.

Published in March 2011
on the Ananias website

THINKING MAKES IT SO?

"There is nothing either good or bad, but thinking makes it so." Anyone who has studied daily from the Christian Science textbook can probably recognize those words from William Shakespeare's *Hamlet* (see Act 2, Sc. 2, line 255).

They appear in *Science and Health* as one of three epigraphs (the author's chosen mottos for the entire book) just behind the title page. They sum up the Christian Science promise that we can think our way to health, happiness, holiness, and heaven. In philosophical and moral terms, they express the height of subjectivism and relativism.

Strangely, however, the epigraph quotations just before and after this one—Jesus' words from John 8:32 about knowing the truth, and a poetic fragment by Mrs. Eddy that begins, "Thou hast heard my prayer"—strongly refute subjectivism and relativism with their affirmation that truth and God are objectively real.

Strangely as well, anyone who asks himself if all good and bad are merely thought up, whether or not he is a Christian Scientist, will have to admit he doesn't believe they are. Nor does he live and act as if they are.

In a little meditation he published for Good Friday, essayist Andrew Klavan reminds us that "Hamlet spoke these words when he was pretending to be insane…[but] the position, as Shakespeare knew, is not only crazy, it's make-believe crazy, because no one actually believes it.

"You can't make the argument for moral truth without God," Klavan points out. "If our conscience matters, it can only be because existence is a person and we are made in that person's image." The image of the three-person God revealed to us in Scripture, that is.

No, thinking doesn't make it "so." The existential reality of God and man, good and evil, sin and salvation, is already so; eternally so.

Words to the contrary, from an imaginary Shakespeare character feigning madness, only serve to embolden the Christian Scientist in hopeless pursuit of self-salvation. Begone with them, then. Begone indeed with the whole Bible-subverting textbook that has lured so many earnest souls down a Hamlet path leading nowhere. Forgive me if it sounds harsh: Begone!

Published in April 2014
on the Ananias website

TYRANNY OF THE INSECURE

What's going on with the hesitancy, or outright self-censorship, felt by many of us in telling our family and friends why we now follow Jesus instead of Mrs. Eddy? Sometimes that reticence may even deter us from going on record publicly about our reasons for leaving Christian Science, out of concern for how someone might be personally wounded by our words. But why?

Two early supporters of the Ananias website, Carol and Nancy, recently declined my invitation to be identified by name on the site. "I would love to shout it from the rooftops," wrote Carol. But then she added that were she to publish "any criticism of Christian Science, my loved ones will feel attacked, and absolutely refuse to hear anything I say. They tend to be very sensitive to any differing opinions."

Nancy, separately but in similar terms, deferred to the sensitivity of her elderly parents, along with her two sisters and their children. "If they were to read the material on Ananias and see my name on it," she said, "it could have caused them some pain, and I didn't want to take the chance of that happening."

Her mother and father are both approaching 90 but doing very well, partly because of "their positive outlook on life, via the Christian Science mindset," Nancy told me, adding: "Who am I to judge them and tell them otherwise?"

Feeling Attacked

What is it about the followers of Christian Science, so certain they are in touch with the "final revelation" of Truth (SH 107:5), that makes them at the same time so susceptible to feeling attacked or experiencing pain if a fellow Scientist—especially a relative—walks away from the faith and politely states his or her reasons?

Why this strange mix of security and insecurity? Why the tendency to take a difference of opinion personally, when Mrs. Eddy calls on students to exclude "personality" and "personal sense" from their thinking?

We can analyze the reasons some other time. What strikes me at present is how one person's thin skin and easily-hurt feelings can tyrannically dominate not only another person's harmless self-honesty, but also the over-sensitive individual's own ability to face reality and reason clearly.

My wife and I, after we learned the ropes in marriage, used to laugh about the way novices in relationships (including our former selves) will manipulate or be manipulated by the self-pitying line, "If you really loved me..." Translation: Be my puppet or you're sentenced to my doghouse. So runs the tyranny of hurt feelings in terms of A pushing around B.

But the worst of such tyranny is the way it imprisons A himself. Like the young man who went away from Jesus sad because he had great possessions (Matthew 19:22), A first stops his ears to the claims of Christ.

He then runs a passive-aggressive guilt trip on family member B for daring to advocate those claims—all of that in order to protect the "great possessions" of A's triumphal but oh-so-fragile *Science and Health* worldview.

It's a trivial cliche, but regrettably apropos: "My mind is made up (about all things religious). Don't upset me with the facts (of how your mind was remade about those very same things)."

May our friends or family who still follow Christian Science be set free by God from the tyranny of hurt feelings. May they show charitable respect, not emotional blackmail, to those of us who have chosen to leave Science, in the spirit of Abram parting amicably with Lot in Genesis 13:7-9.

And having done so, may they then approach with calm clarity the choices that will determine their own eternal destiny.

Published in October 2010
on the Ananias website

A GRANDSON'S PRAYER

Adam, a young businessman nearing 30, raised as an evangelical Christian, thoughtful, well-read, and free-spirited, contacted me recently at the suggestion of a mutual friend. He was concerned about his grandmother, Carolyn, nearing 80, a lifelong Christian Scientist married to an agnostic, and now facing grave health concerns.

I took Adam to lunch. Knowing I had come to the Cross from Christian Science at about age 40, he wanted help making sense of Carolyn's dogged resistance to both the skeptical arguments of her husband and the biblical appeals of himself as a grandson. (Also the appeals of a son, since Adam's father is an evangelical too.)

What is it about Mrs. Eddy's system, Adam asked, that can take such an unshakable hold on someone like his grandmother? His eyes got big when I showed and explained to him *Science and Health with Key to the Scriptures*, which he had never seen before.

130

We talked about the power of the system's claim to be scientific, and the high ground seized by its pretension of being the Bible's only reliable interpreter. The latter claim is clinched by the textbook's "Glossary" chapter, I pointed out, and the former by the "Fruitage" chapter.

Adam said that his psychology-professor grandfather, Herb, endlessly objects that a real science would study and acknowledge its failures as well as its successes, but Carolyn brushes that off. I concurred that no accounts of healings not achieved appear in "Fruitage," nor are such matters taken up in the Scientists' testimony meetings or the periodicals.

The copy of Mrs. Eddy's book that I had brought to lunch happened to be one where I have marked every Bible quotation or allusion in the entire book, hundreds of them in all. Adam began to see how the massive combined weight of scriptural references and distortions—buttressed with the group-think of "it must be true, it heals"—weaves a web of plausibility and confident Gnostic belonging around good people like Carolyn.

Suspensions of Logic

But what about his grandmother's lifelong reliance on dentistry and eyeglasses, my friend wanted to know: how does that square with the professed standard of health care by spiritual means alone? Of course it doesn't.

Yet by such suspensions of logic and common sense, grown numbingly familiar during more than a century (six generations in some families), has the system eased its rigidity just enough to permit continuance of the self-reinforcing mentality of acceptance that carries a believer along.

Nonetheless, Adam told me, a recent severe illness had so frightened Carolyn that she yielded to Herb's pleading for a medical diagnosis, underwent hospitalization, and—at the time of our conversation—was cooperating with a course of blood treatments prescribed as vital to her survival.

The young man praised God for this much opening-up on his grandmother's part. But as we ended the lunch, he said his continuing prayer is for her to renounce Christian Science not just medically but theologically—and from there, come to a saving knowledge of Jesus Christ before she leaves this world. In which prayer we can all join.

Published in April 2007
on the Ananias website

TALKING PAST EACH OTHER

What might Christian Scientists learn from evangelical Christians, especially as it relates to fostering church growth? Doesn't Mrs. Eddy's church manual suggest friendliness between her followers and evangelicals?

These questions surfaced out of a Christian Science luncheon group after some of them discovered they shared an appreciation of one of the popular preachers often seen on television. A participant in the conversation, knowing that this particular broadcast is often part of breakfast at my house, messaged me about it.

The reply I sent her was couched mildly and obliquely, hoping to elicit a dialogue. I wanted to avoid seeming to trump this friend's (mis)understanding of the subject with my own pronouncements. So I wrote as follows:

> Your report of the lunch discussion sent me to the concordance for Mrs. Eddy's writings. There I found a couple of dozen references in all, from her textbook and other works, to 'evangelical' and related words. These contained various hints about the questions you asked me, but nothing definitive.

Judging from all the citations taken together, it seems to me your elderly guest, the lady in her 90s, was right — Mrs. Eddy hoped to be on friendly terms with evangelical churches and believers but found it difficult.

The only *Manual* reference is page 17:5, which suggests the early members of her church saw themselves as pilgrims making an exodus out of evangelical churches to seek something they were missing. The implication was that of two paths diverging, not that of convergence.

The citation most striking to me is from *Science and Health* on page 254, 'The human self must be evangelized.' The verb there means, according to a contemporary dictionary, brought to accept one's salvation from sin through the atoning death of Jesus.

That's interesting, because in thinking back, I realize this is precisely what made me an evangelical Christian. They taught this definition of salvation — whereas Christian Science did not do so at all.

I think it was my frustrations and failings as a husband that convinced me I'm a sinner in need of a savior. There is a practical realism in someone like the TV preacher you asked about, which I just don't find in *Science and Health*, in terms of facing up to our human flaws and seeking the compassionate redemption of those by the crucified and risen Christ.

So that's what I told her, hoping to nudge the discussion along. But as so often happens, when she wrote me back, it became clear my Christian Science friend and I were talking right past each other. The sharp theological divergence I was hoping to illustrate from personal experience, seemed lost on her.

She had the childlike assumption, so common among Mrs. Eddy's followers, that differences between biblical Christianity and

Christian Science are little more than shadings—though always showing the superiority of the latter—rather than diametric opposition at crucial points as is really the case.

She didn't even know what she didn't know. I pray each day for her and others like her, that God through his Son and his Spirit will bring them to know!

Published in February 2009
on the Ananias website

DOWN THE GENERATIONS

There's one piece of writing that I did, related to the themes in this book though longer than most of the essays here, that is not included in the collection. It explores in fictional form the question of how Mrs. Eddy's "spiritual children," if you will, have turned out, today a century later.

It came to be written because I found myself struggling, as a newer follower of Jesus, with seeing objectively into my own mental landscape and life experience as Christian Science had shaped them. I felt the need to do this for two reasons.

First, stepping away from long-familiar thought patterns toward freedom in Christ was going to take a conscious effort. And secondly, reaching out to Scientists with what I now knew of the gospel would require all the empathy I could muster about how things looked from the inside, seen through their eyes.

So as a way of getting my own religious and cultural background "out there where I could take a look at it," I got the idea of sketching an imaginary Christian Science family's story across a number of years.

This could all be told in a few paragraphs, I thought. Not quite: the result actually ran to several thousand words. I wrote it in 1998, five years after I was baptized, 18 years after I accepted Christ. Start to poke around in an attic, and there is often a lot more in there than we expect.

Opportunities and Obstacles

The piece was eventually published as a booklet with the title *Mrs. Eddy's Children: A Five-Generation Portrait*. I benefited a great deal from writing it, in just the ways I had hoped. I still get new insights — about who I am and have been, and about opportunities and obstacles for evangelizing the MBE followers today — each time I read through this story.

Mrs. Eddy's Children is simply a narrative told from the outside. It does not argue doctrine, pass judgment, or draw conclusions. It aims for a fair and mild tone, granting this fictional family of Scientists, the Walkers, the respect I believe they deserve.

And to repeat, the entire story is imaginary. No person or incident in my life, or known to me, is disguised there. I hope it may prove beneficial to readers whether they are current Christian Scientists, former Christian Scientists, or inquirers about Christian Science.

My own gratitude to God does increase, however, each time I relive the Andrews family's actual multi-generational encounter with the alluring but ultimately unfulfilling Eddy way of life — three generations before my own who devoutly followed it, and now three generations including my own who have gratefully left it behind.

The faithfulness of the Father, whether glimpsed through a glass darkly or seen face to face, has never failed my wife and me and our children and grandson. Never. I echo, on behalf of us all, the Psalmist's grateful words: "The lines are fallen to [us] in pleasant places; [we] have a goodly heritage" (Psalm 16:6).

Note: If you're interested, *Mrs. Eddy's Children* can be ordered through a link on the Ananias.org homepage.

Published in February 2010
on the Ananias website

THE NARROW GATE

Why should any intelligent adult have to ask someone else's permission before making up their mind about whether the Bible is true? They shouldn't. There's no need.

But that is essentially the position of some Christian Scientists, followers of Mrs. Eddy who have begun to doubt her teachings yet continue to feel emotionally beholden to her. Stirred by Christ's call of "Come," they are seemingly compelled to ask her, "Should I?" It makes no sense.

To assess this compulsion, we need to put in perspective the two books that Scientists study daily, hear from in church, and regard as their pastor.

In the ancient world over the course of centuries, some forty men who personally knew Jesus of Nazareth—or spiritually foresaw him—wrote book after book about this "only begotten Son of God" and his Father, the almighty Creator of all things.

As growing multitudes began to acclaim Jesus as God incarnate, Savior and Lord, apostolic followers collected the most reliable writings about who he was, how he came and way, 66 documents in all, into one great holy book, the Bible. For 1500 years it stood as the definitive account of creation and redemption, good and evil, truth and lies, life and love: the meaning of everything.

Then in the modern world in 1875 one woman—one woman—wrote a book undertaking to correct and perfect the

Bible, all of Christian history and belief to the contrary notwithstanding. This audacious prophetess was Mary Baker Eddy, author of the Christian Science textbook, *Science and Health with Key to the Scriptures.*

Wanting Reassurance

Most of the world took no notice. But for some of us who grew up under its influence and spent many years of our lives steeped in it, *Science and Health* came to exert an iron grip over our conception of who God is and how we should relate to him; far more than the Bible.

Objectively there is no justification for this, considering the relative weight of the two books' truth-claims. But subjectively, the textbook's hold can seem almost unbreakable.

So even as these questioning Scientists feel Jesus drawing them in, they seem unable to move toward him decisively — rooted to the spot, as it were; looking back over their shoulder for some reassurance that Christian Science indeed sheds valuable new light on the things of God.

They're hesitant to enter the Body of Christ unless Mrs. Eddy can come with them. They comb her writings for a rationale to justify this. It's as if their identity and self-worth are at stake in vindicating, at least partially, the "beloved leader" they've followed for so long.

Hw do I know? Because this was me. This "stuck place" was exactly where I was for years before finally giving my heart to Jesus in 1980, and for more than a decade thereafter.

It took me that long to realize that I didn't need Mary Baker Eddy's permission to believe the Holy Scriptures on their own terms — that I was actually choking myself with intellectualism and spiritual pride by obsessing about her.

Enter Alone

"Enter now, John, and enter alone." That's what I seemed to hear the Lord saying at last. He calls himself, after all, the door, the gate, the way; indeed the one and only way. Trying to enter hand in hand with anyone — my wife or my children or my dad or Mrs. Eddy — wasn't going to work, I saw. The gate is too narrow for that.

As for any "key" to truth or salvation or life eternal, the Bible assigns that key specifically to Jesus Christ in Revelation, chapters 1 and 3.

We also read of him entrusting it to the apostolic succession through Peter in Matthew 16. But nothing is said of a key in some far-off future book. Rather the closing words of Revelation 22 (and hence of the entire Bible) warn us away from such purported scriptural add-ons.

I began to lose interest in vindicating Mrs. Eddy, the more I reflected on the anomaly, or blasphemy, of a writer who would consciously contradict Scripture in purporting to unlock it.

As Jesus explains to Peter in Matthew 19:27-30, forsaking all to follow him is a stern requirement but at the same time a wondrous offer — since the reborn believer in due time finds "more than all" restored to him. It certainly proved so for me.

'Yes But'

Finally relinquishing, after a long struggle, the valued insights I had clung to in the textbook and the filial loyalty I had for its author, I was recompensed a hundredfold with Scripture's pure truths and the Lord's personal love for me, exactly as he promised.

Whether we look at that Matthew 19 story of the rich young ruler, or the excuses made to Jesus in Luke chapters 9 and 14, the warning for a stuck-in-the-middle doubter of Christian Science is the same. The only answer to our Lord's invitation of "Come" is to come, period. Telling him "yes but" is the same as telling him "no."

And what a price we pay for that "but." What a costly and needless postponement — or worse, a forever loss — of the precious pearl he offers the humble, the obedient, the surrendered.

The unsurrendered one, the excuse-maker, for a long time was me, as I said. Is it now you?

Don't wait or hesitate, my friend, for anyone's permission to embrace without reservations the King of Kings and his Book of Books. Don't!

The decision is yours alone. Make it today. You have nothing of substance to lose, and eternity to gain.

Published in January 2017
on the Ananias website

St. Paul disputing with the philosophers on Mars Hill (Dore)

CHAPTER 7:
COULD WE TRY TALKING IT OVER?

Having a dialogue about the things of God with someone deeply committed to Christian Science is not easy. For me as one who left the fold, it's harder still. Though courtesy usually prevails, I feel silently judged as a deserter and suspected as a sower of doubt. Yet with so much more to gain than lose, I keep trying.

THE DARE

"Lord, what wilt thou have me to do?" The imploring question to Jesus from Saul of Tarsus in Acts 9:6 has heavily burdened me of late.

On my heart are several earnest seekers for an exit out of Christian Science. I've been pondering and praying over how to help them pass over the last bridge they can't seem to cross in fully breaking with Mrs. Eddy and submitting to Jesus Christ as Savior and Lord.

Reviewing my conversations with some of these "almost out, but stuck" Christian Scientists, I saw there are four questions we ask ourselves in working out our religion, worldview, and way of life.

1. What do I want from others?

2. What do others want from me?

3. What do I want from God?

4. What does God want from me?

And I realized how much easier the first three questions are for all of us as fallen human beings to grapple with and eventually answer — compared to that last question, which is truly the ultimate issue in anyone's life.

Specifically with the Christian Science mindset, which teaches us to think of God as an idea, an impersonal bundle of attributes and synonyms, a metaphysically and mentally accessible "something," it is all too easy for the restless yet comfortable Christian Scientist to leave God in a vague status where "wanting this or that from me" isn't even a meaningful concept.

All Relative, All Subjective

Put differently: by relativizing and subjectivizing all reality, the Eddy teachings temptingly invite followers—even when inclined to leave Science as such—to make God in their own convenient image rather than bow in submission as His fallen but forgiven image.

So my fourth question, the ultimate question with all its risk and discomfort and unsettling consequences, hovers out there beyond the horizon, so much easier to evade and dodge than to confront and face the music.

<u>What does God want from me?</u> My all, everything I am and have and value and hope for. The whole thing, nothing held back.

<u>And who is this all-demanding God?</u> Not merely seven synonyms, but none other than the triune Father, Son, and Holy Spirit whom first, imperfectly, the Jews glimpsed and served and whom now for twenty centuries the Christians have fully known (but also, in their own way, imperfectly served) through Jesus of Nazareth, crucified and risen, ascended and reigning.

<u>And where do we meet this narrowly particular God?</u> In the pages of his written word, the Bible, and in the lives of his saints, and in the long unbroken (though again imperfect) stewardship of his church.

Even as I typed the previous dozen lines, I could hear the almost-out-but-stuck Christian Scientist, gripped more strongly than he can possibly know by intellectual self-sovereignty, saying "Yes, but…."

The Last Bridge

It's a neat evasion on the part of these intellectually facile Christian Scientists, all the neater because naively unconscious, to keep postponing the Saul of Tarsus moment of reckoning with a stern but loving God by hiding behind faux-sophisticated definitional and epistemological quibbles over which God exactly are we talking about and how can we be sure anyway.

Boiled down, that moment of hesitation followed by their umpteenth refusal to cross over, amounts to the wavering Scientist having been given a dare, weighing it briefly, and then yet again saying No. The same dare as so often before. But always the same No.

Father, give me prayerful patience and persistence to stay in dialogue with these loved ones—and give each the humbling lessons that will push him or her across the final, difficult, glorious bridge from almost-out to fully-out. That some bright day they will once more hear the dare and at last say—Yes!

Published in August 2017
on the Ananias website

WES BACKS AWAY

Relying on a textbook they call the Key to the Scriptures and on six tenets that seem to uphold the Scriptures, many faithful Christian Scientists are unaware of how radically their religion reinterprets the Bible and how sharply it departs from the historic consensus of Protestant, Catholic, and Orthodox theology.

Wes, whom I've known since we were Adventure Unlimited camp counselors together in the 1960s, is a good example. He wrote to ask about some college memories I'd posted on my political blog.

After describing my time at Principia College as "four of the best years of my life," I added that I later "had another great four years working as a vice president at Hillsdale, to which I must regretfully give the edge over my beloved Principia in terms of conservative principles and fidelity to biblical truth."

Wes's question was this: "I concur with your judgment that Hillsdale stands out in terms of conservative principles, but I was mystified as to your comment choosing Hillsdale over Principia for fidelity to biblical truth. Could you give me an example?"

Which Book to Believe

Notice that my friend wasn't saying he knew what I likely meant and that he'd probably disagree, pending my statement of the case. He was declaring himself mystified. My email reply went this way:

> Wes, thanks for your note. This is not a new thing in my life, but I guess we've never talked about it. In the early '80s, after much struggle, I found there was more help and comfort in the Bible if I read it on its own terms rather than through the lens of *Science and Health*.
>
> Above all, this was the case in understanding what it meant that Christ died for my sins. Reluctantly I faced a choice between Mrs. Eddy and her book, and Jesus and his book. I chose the latter, and it was the greatest event of my life. Principia obviously comes down on the MBE side.
>
> I have only charitable feelings toward Christian Science and its church, as well as toward Prin as my alma mater, as expressed in the blog post you asked about. But this was the reason I left the employment of Adventure Unlimited in 1981 and ended up working for Hillsdale. I resigned from the Mother Church in 1992 and have been active as a Presbyterian since then. Glad you asked.

Factually, I wanted to give Wes the information he deserved as an old friend. Spiritually, I wanted to speak the truth to him in love, hoping to start a dialogue and ultimately open his eyes to the Gospel. I could only await his reply and then see if my frank and friendly approach would get anywhere.

Five Words

I knew if we did have a dialogue, one obstacle would be the Christian Scientists' rejection of traditionally understood biblical terms and claims. Take the text I cited from I Corinthians 15:3, "Christ died for our sins." Difficulties with *all five* of those words arise from Mary Baker Eddy's vocabulary and doctrine.

1. She says Christ is an idea, undying and distinct from the man Jesus.

2. She says that in any event, Jesus himself while in the tomb was not really dead either.

3. She rejects the notion of a substitionary atonement, whereby the Lord's crucifixion and resurrection occurred in our place or "for" us.

4. She declares sin to be unreal, an illusion or false belief.

5. Even this illusory condition can't actually be "ours" (or "mine," as I wrote to Wes), since according to Mrs. Eddy each of us has only the sinless nature we possess as God's spiritual reflection; we have no other identity to which sin could attach.

Five simple words, one of the most momentous and famous sentences in the Bible, and when a Jesus follower says them, an Eddy follower hears the same sounds but receives an entirely different meaning. No wonder the saved Christian and the scientific Christian have trouble understanding each other.

The experience I had at about age 40, as briefly described to Wes above, was a convergence of powerful new insights from two sources: a more honest knowledge of myself and a truer perspective on the Bible.

I became convinced, from what I saw inside me and around me, that I was a sinner in need of a Savior. Then I was tremendously encouraged to find in Scripture (as I read it for the first time without letting *Science and Health* get in the way) the good news of that very Savior, through such passages as I Corinthians 15:3 and many others.

Evasive

The tragedy of Christian Science is that it seems to render a determined adherent such as Wes, virtually deaf and blind to both the awareness of his need and the availability of Christ's answer.

St. Paul, writing further to the Corinthians, speaks of the challenge he and his coworkers faced, as "able ministers of the new testament," in evangelizing the Jews, whose "minds were blinded" by unbelief in the Messiah, so that "until this day remaineth the same veil untaken away in the reading of the old testament" (II Corinthians 3:6, 14).

A similar veiling of both testaments obstructs the evangelizing of Christian Scientists today. Paul assures us, though, that the veil "is done away in Christ," and two verses later he repeats that when the unbeliever's "heart…shall turn to the Lord, the veil shall be taken away."

There's no reason Wes can't experience that turn of heart, and with it the unobscured view of Scripture that I received by God's grace years ago. But for now, it's clear he and I need have no further dialogue. He answered my email the next day, writing as follows:

> Thanks for your clear explanation. I have always valued you as a friend and as a perceptive thinker and continue to do so. I understand (more clearly with each passing year it seems) that each of us have to find our own way through life's grand adventure.
>
> I am presently communicating with a young man who worked for me during college and while studying to be a minister. He married, had a couple of kids and was pastor at a Presbyterian church. But he had an affair, quit his pastorate, divorced his wife,

and next week he is getting married to the other woman and they are coming to visit our town.

I confess to struggling to understand the choices he has made and the wreckage left behind. But we'll probably meet when he's here, because I know him as a good and decent man whom I count continue to count a good friend. At times like this I just ask myself, "What would Jesus do?"

There are a number of ways to read this. But I decided not to spend much time on it, let alone ask Wes to clarify. Better to drop the matter for now, as it was obvious he's rather not engage on the touchy (to him, not to me) question of why I left Christian Science and why he hasn't.

But how the sexually fallen pastor got into the discussion certainly isn't clear. Was it because this troubled individual is, like me, a Presbyterian? Or did this man's "finding his own way through life's grand adventure" somehow remind Wes of my choosing a different path as well, as though our two stories were somehow comparable?

I'll Keep Praying

As for the "What would Jesus do?" cliché, does that too signal that I and the divorcing pastor are to be equally forgiven, incomprehensible as our respective actions may be in Wes's mind? Not that I'd feel offended by this implication; but if true, it says something about the hermetically sealed world of doctrinal certainty in which many Scientists live.

On the other hand, maybe Wes meant to imply no judgment on me at all, but merely sought to illustrate that we both follow Jesus with equal fidelity. Nearly all Scientists utterly believe that about themselves—missing the crucial distinction between the Savior we meet in Scripture and the Way-shower or Examplar whom Mrs. Eddy proclaims (SH 497:15 and 5:31).

In any case, two things are plain from what Wes wrote about "each finding his own way."

He didn't accept the exclusivity of Jesus' statement that "no man cometh unto the Father, but by me" and of Peter's confirming assertion that "there is none other name given under heaven among men [but that of Jesus Christ], whereby we must be saved" (John 14:6 and Acts 4:12).

Nor, on the other hand, did my friend seem to accept the exclusivity of Mrs. Eddy's bold prediction in 1902 that "Christian Science is destined to be the one and the only religion and therapeutics on this planet" (*Miscellany* 266:29).

Or perhaps he did accept the latter and simply preferred not to talk about how it's all expected to work out for such stragglers as the apostate pastor and me.

No matter. My task is simply to keep praying for Wes and all the Christian Scientists to find "the Way, the Truth, and the Life" in the Man of Galilee as I did.

Published in September 2008
on the Ananias website

JACK TAKES THE PLUNGE

Excitement ran high this fall as Americans elected a president. But Jack Norman, a New England man in his fifties, will remember those weeks in September and October not so much for the political headlines as for his new birth in Jesus Christ.

Jack was raised in Christian Science, wandered away in his late teens, came back to it briefly a decade ago, then left forever without finding another spiritual anchor for his life. Along the way, he watched both parents die fairly young — and needlessly, he felt—under Christian Science treatment, lost his first wife to alcoholism, raised their children, and built a business.

Then several months ago, something drew Jack to the Christian Way website, and from there to the Ananias website. He contacted me to learn more, and from this an acquaintance sprang up. He told me of his hunger to really know God, saying, "I feel about eight years old spiritually."

Jack said he had begun reading the Bible with new eyes, digging into books like Lee Strobel's *The Case for Christ* and John Stott's *Basic Christianity*, learning to pray daily, and visiting local churches with Kelly, his current wife, looking for something that seemed right for them.

On the last weekend in October, Jack felt the time had come to give his life entirely to Jesus. You can imagine the rejoicing with which I received this news. Jack's initial email to me had stated:

> The biggest problem I think I have, something I learned in Christian Science as a child, is that problems aren't real. As a result I tend to procrastinate and live in denial far too much of the time. This has caused some significant problems in my life—and continues to do so.
>
> In terms of Christianity, I definitely consider myself a Christian. But I only attend church on Christmas and Easter and frequently try out different churches. I am happily remarried and have a successful business, but I do feel that there is a void in my life.

Accepted the Invitation

I told Jack that such a "void" was something I too had experienced, as have countless others before they came to know the Lord. It is the "God-shaped hole in each person's heart" about which St. Augustine wrote 1600 years ago. The dialogue continued. Recently he wrote as follows about the climactic autumn day at a nearby college:

> God continues to call me to His service and, in fact, on Saturday afternoon, just after completing the penultimate chapter in *Basic Christianity* and having been challenged by Dr. Stott to make a decision about Christ, I knelt in front of a beautiful pond on the campus and recited the prayer that Dr. Stott recommended.
>
> I accepted the invitation to "Believe on the Lord Jesus Christ, and thou shalt be saved" (Acts 16:31). I had begun to feel pretty certain that I was going to be born again and was patiently waiting for the right time—"Thy will be done." I had left Kelly with her son and was walking alone, thinking about the fact that I had one more chapter of Stott to read but it was only to be read by believers in Christ.
>
> I knew I had become one but I still had to physically kneel before Him and declare my commitment to Him; to answer His knock on the door that had been barred to His entry all these years and welcome Christ into my life forever. It was a beautiful, glorious moment and I am aware that my life will never be the same.

If you are in circumstances at all similar to those of Jack Norman, as a result of having earlier followed Christian Science or any other non-biblical teaching and now wanting to know God better—if you would like to experience the life-changing new relationship and fresh start that Jack described—I urge you to act on that impulse. An open door awaits you, and as Jack said, your life will never be the same.

Published in November 2008
on the Ananias website

DIMINISHING JESUS

Anyone who says the way to have more truth and more life is to diminish Jesus Christ, is going to have a fight on their hands with me. Over the years, with no ill will toward my Christian Science friends, I have come to see that this is exactly what their doctrine leads to: a smaller Jesus.

It becomes especially clear at the two peaks of the Christian year, Christmas and Easter. These holy days dramatize how Mary Baker Eddy, for some reason (whether her motives were benign or malign I don't know, and it doesn't matter), inverted the great precept of John the Baptist in John 3:30. That is, she decreed in effect that Jesus must decrease and she herself must increase.

Take for example her well-known verses entitled "Blest Christmas Morn," appointed to be sung often as a hymn in Christian Science churches (*Christian Science Hymnal*, No. 23). That hymn *lessens* Christmas by diminishing and demoting the baby of Bethlehem in almost every one of its twenty lines.

We are given to understand that neither the child in the manger nor man on the cross stands nearly as high in Mrs. Eddy's theology as her eternal impersonal Christ, a deathless "God-idea" or "gentle beam" of immaterial concepts. We're left wondering why the birth of Mary's child really mattered at all to us mortals.

I had an amicable but disappointing conversation about this the other day with Ted, an earnest Christian Science friend of mine. Ted is touchingly open to biblical truth unfiltered through the Eddy textbook, and it's clear he loves Jesus. That love goes only so far, however, for Ted remains doggedly loyal to Mrs. Eddy's metaphysical rewrite of the gospel.

Grasping for some persuasive way to challenge his illogic, I realized how much my own early doubts about Science, decades ago, had owed to the chilly abstractions that assault us in "Blest Christmas Morn."

The hymn, along with other compelling factors, had finally led me to ask myself a series of simple questions. I now in turn asked those same questions of Ted.

1. Whom do you love more, Mrs. Eddy or Jesus?

2. Who apparently loves Jesus more, you or Mrs. Eddy?

3. On the evidence of their writings and statements, does Mrs. Eddy love Jesus as much as, or more than, John the Baptist, or Matthew, Mark, Luke, and John, or Peter and Paul?

4. Or does she apparently love him less than do those saints (a word puzzlingly and inaptly used at the close of "Blest Christmas Morn," by the way—further diminishing Jesus)?

5. And if she does love him less than they do, why place any reliance on her words and example in preference to their words and example?

I never received any answer to these questions from my friend Ted. In God's own time, however, I still may. I pray it will be the answer I gave our Lord in song on that Christmas long ago: "My Jesus, I love thee, I know thou art mine."

Published in December 2016
on the Ananias website

MUCH TO ATONE FOR

Recently a friend asked me to attend her Christian Science church service. The lesson was on "Doctrine of Atonement." Twice a year for forty years, prior to leaving Science, I had studied this at home for a solid week, and sat through it in church on Sunday, without — I realized that day — ever asking myself why Mrs. Eddy addressed it in a chapter of *Science and Health* and made it a lesson-sermon subject.

So why was it? My conclusion now is that she was explaining it only to explain it away, as part of her audacious attempt to recast 1800 years of Christian theology, and Scripture itself.

But it got me to thinking about some questions we could ask the Christian Scientist as a point of entry into (unlikely but not impossible) mutual understanding. Such questions as:

- Have you ever done anything you needed to atone for? Anything you couldn't atone for? What was the outcome of that?

- When you look in the mirror, do you see a sinner? If not, do you see someone who is flawed, fallible, less than perfect? How is that different from being a sinner?

- Are you, as I am, often aware of displeasing God? And sometimes greatly displeasing him? What's your solution to that? Mine is based on "Christ died for our sins," Paul's gospel in I Corinthians 15:3, referencing Isaiah. But you as a Christian Scientist must have a different solution, since the atonement chapter in your textbook says Jesus didn't "relieve [us] of a single responsibility" (SH 18:9).

- Would it be fair to say Science just teaches you can think your way from a wrong relationship with God into a right one? How confident are you of that approach for daily life now and for eternal life in the future? How permanent are the results? Is there a "hold" function on the mental work you do, so it locks in and doesn't lapse back?

- In that the first tenet of Christian Science (SH 497:3) affirms the reliability of the Bible, why don't you accept that Jesus died for our sins? If he didn't die for our sins, why did he die?

- Or do you even believe he really died? Mrs. Eddy after all, states categorically that there is no death, and she specifically says Jesus "had not died" (SH 46:3, see also 44:28). Then again, in her metaphysics, sin is no more real than death or hell — so what need is there of atonement for sin anyway?

Well, my list of questions could go on, but you get the idea. In imagining a dialogue of this kind, I'm not trying for the easy satisfaction of winning a debate, but for the genuine exploration of thought with an earnest Scientist who believes "the time for thinkers has come" (SH vii:13).

Which is, as I said, uncommon given the closed circularity of that belief system — but it's still worth trying for. And this approach of building a ladder of honest, respectful, fact-finding questions to engage the occasional open-minded Christian Scientist feels promising to me. I'm going to keep working on it.

Published in October 2017
on the Ananias website

WHY SETTLE FOR LESS?

Wouldn't you want the *whole* Bible, every verse of its truth, every word of its love — and not just parts of it? This is one of several basic questions I'd like to ask a faithful Christian Scientist if he or she were willing to discuss things with an open heart and mind. Another would be:

Wouldn't you want *all* of Christ Jesus, Jesus in his fullness as God incarnate, Savior and Lord, conquering King, crucified and risen and alive today, reigning at the right hand of the Father where he ever intercedes for us — and not a lesser Jesus, stripped of his divinity?

And then this question: What are you missing in the Bible, what are you missing in Jesus, when you accept a diminished substitute for the entirety of both across two millennia — a substitute propounded by one Boston woman barely a century ago?

As hard as it may be for you to accept (I imagine myself saying), the only way to have the Son of God in full and the Scriptures in full is to follow Christianity in full as a wholehearted Protestant or Catholic or Orthodox believer — all are equally valid — and cease following Mary Baker Eddy.

No Gatekeeper Needed

Yes, I'm saying *break off* with Christian Science — in order to engage with God's Word and God's Son as never before; in order to come to the Cross of Christ. Or do you feel no need of that?

Think how much you love God as Life, Truth, and Love; as Principle, Mind, Soul, and Spirit. More than words can say, right? To know the depth and breadth of His all-acting self-expression as Mind or Principle, you wouldn't want to miss a single page of the Bible from Genesis to Revelation, would you?

To see all the way into what Jesus was claiming with his "I am" statement about personally being Truth and Life (John 14:6), you wouldn't want to take anyone's word for it but his own about who he was, would you? Yet Mrs. Eddy interposes herself as gate-keeper there. Are you content with that?

I was content with it for many years. But there came a time when, as a Sunday school teacher for teens at our branch church, I wanted to help them take Jesus more seriously—and realized I ought to take him more seriously myself.

Then while serving as First Reader a few years later, I began to see as never before what a treasure the Bible is. Confining my study within the blue chalk lines didn't seem adequate for really searching the Scriptures as Jesus commanded (John 5:39). "There is more here," I realized.

How much more, I never dreamed. You can find what I found, what many of us have found, but only by inquiring and exploring and seeing for yourself. What's stopping you?

Published in August 2012
on the Ananias website

WEIGH THE EVIDENCE

A Christian Scientist I hadn't known very well, a younger guy named Doug, asked me why it was that I left Christian Science years ago. I sensed he was open to a full and honest explanation. He sincerely wanted to know, for his own benefit.

So we met for lunch, and after briefly setting the background of my spiritual journey, I told Doug that for me, it had all come down to three simple but momentous questions. Each has a couple of possible answers.

1. *Who is Jesus?*
   a. A good man

    b.   The God-man

2. *Who am I?*
    a.   Perfect
    b.   Imperfect

3. *Who is the church?*
    a.   All the followers of Mrs. Eddy since 1866
    b.   All the followers of Jesus since AD 30

Christian Science says Jesus is just a good man — the best man ever, but nothing more; certainly not Deity incarnate. But evidence in the Bible and events in the 1st century say he is the God-man, and I finally became persuaded of that evidence.

Christian Science says I am perfect, and any suggestion to the contrary is merely a false dream (though how my perfection could undergo any such dream isn't explained). But evidence from my own self-knowledge and experience says I am imperfect, and I finally became persuaded of that evidence as well.

The two strands of evidence in fact reinforced each other. The more I faced up to my woeful imperfection, the more I needed Jesus as not just my ideal exemplar, but as my divine Savior. The less I resisted his claims as God the Son, who died for me and rose for me, the less I needed to insist (against all reason) upon my sinless perfection.

Flood of Relief

I told Doug the flood of relief and rightness that I felt in finally coming home, coming in from the cold, made the whole thing for me not so much a matter of "leaving" Christian Science but more a matter of "joining" God's royal household after a lifetime away.

That brings us to the third question: Who is the church? Christian Science confines it narrowly to the followers of Mrs. Eddy since 1866. But evidence in the Bible and events in twenty centuries ever since, define it broadly as all the followers of Jesus since AD 30.

That widely inclusive royal household, which is labeled as 3b in my list of questions, has agreed throughout the ages with the theological positions I've labeled 1b and 2b.

How could the church have endured as it has through the ages, against all odds, without a burning conviction that Jesus is the God-man? And how could someone as imperfect as I know myself to be, dare reject the church's certainty in favor of my own uncertainty? And why, in the vulnerability that comes with imperfection, exclude myself from Jesus' family

"So it all lines up, Doug," I concluded in my conversation with this young inquirer, a man who happens to make his living evaluating evidence. Regard yourself as perfect if you want, I told him. Regard Jesus as just a good man if you want. Regard all the Christians prior to 1866 as mistaken if you want.

But weigh the evidence long and hard before you conclude on those three points; for in each case I have found the evidence decisive on the other side, the Gospel side.

As for that overwhelming sense of welcome when you finally come in from the cold, the sheer rightness of it — words can hardly do it justice. It's just something you have to experience for yourself, my friend.

Published in March 2012
on the Ananias website

PATHWAYS FOR DIALOGUE

"You need Jesus. More than anything, you need Jesus. Your whole life depends on it, your whole world." When I came to accept that this was true and began to make all the changes it would require of me, I was an earnest, fourth-generation Christian Scientist in my late thirties.

It has made a tremendous difference for me ever since, and naturally I have yearned to help other Scientists come to the same realization. Over the decades I have found out how difficult it is to get even the most seemingly open-minded Christian Scientist started down that road, however.

Recently I've begun trying to map out the starting points for receptivity to biblical Christianity that were present in my thinking when Jesus initially made a claim on me.

By reconstructing that long-ago state of mind in which the gospel was able to take hold, maybe I can formulate a more productive approach to those usually-disappointing conversations with Christian Scientists who seem to be, but turn out not to be, open to the invitation of "Think anew."

What I Took Seriously

The starting points, in my case, were four in number. My upbringing in a devout Christian Science family, attending Christian Science schools and camps, studying the weekly lesson and periodicals, attending Sunday and Wednesday services, relying on practitioners, had brought me to take <u>God</u> seriously, take the <u>Bible</u> seriously, take <u>church</u> seriously, and yes, even to take <u>sin</u> seriously. (If that last one sounds unlikely, I'll explain.)

What I didn't take very seriously at all, on the other hand, was history or eternity, or heaven and hell.

And I took myself far too seriously, in terms of a now laughable — but also pitiable — overconfidence that I could think my way, with Mrs. Eddy's help, out of almost any undesirable situation and into almost any desirable situation that might come along.

Because I was a metaphysician, after all. I knew how to give treatments. I knew *Science and Health* almost line by line, and what could resist that kind of spiritual firepower?

So there you have the mental landscape of young John Andrews, circa 1980. Four realities taken quite seriously, albeit imperfectly understood; another four realities not taken seriously enough, albeit superficially acknowledged; and one outsized intellect presiding over them all.

How then did things play out, ultimately leading to my kneeling with two Christian friends and tearfully asking Jesus to be enthroned in my heart?

What Others Shrugged Off

The answer starts with a closer look at what I mean by "taking seriously," or not, those essential concepts mentioned above. Perhaps it will be clearer if we look first at the opposite state of mind — doubt, disregard, dismissal, indifference.

More and more Americans in the years since World War II, my lifetime, are inclined to shrug at God or any other deity, shrug at the Bible and all sacred writings, shrug or shudder at the church as a vessel of holiness and authority, and brush off the idea of sin as a source of guilt and an occasion for punishment.

In contrast, I as a Christian Scientist strongly disagreed with all of those impious attitudes. Any Christian Scientist in 1940 or 1980 or today would say the same.

Is God real and worthy of our devotion? Yes. Is the Bible his inspired word? Yes again. Is the church (allowing for denominational differences) divinely ordained and, as such, the most important of all human institutions? Certainly.

And is the tendency to err, disobey, and rebel — that is, to sin against our Maker — present in all of us and fraught with awful consequences? Certainly again. (Granted, Christian Scientists say sin is unreal, yet they are constantly at war with inward and outward rule-breaking, thus in fact taking sin, as I said, seriously.)

These are the four affirmations that I call my starting points for beginning to grapple — as I did throughout the 1980s — with the gospel of Jesus Christ as God incarnate, crucified, risen, ascended, reigning at the Father's right hand, interceding for us, and one day to return.

God, the Bible, the Church, and the Sin Problem

By no means, at the outset, did I know God truly or fully, but I took him seriously enough to desire to do so.

Likewise my serious engagement with the Bible set the stage for my finding Mrs. Eddy's distortions of it more and more intolerable. Likewise my quest for Christ's _true_ church.

Likewise my ever-increasing horror at the darkness I saw within myself — sins too monstrous for mere metaphysical denial.

History and Eternity, Heaven and Hell

As for the realities I didn't at first take seriously enough, consider _history_ first. How could human beings actually be sinless, "God's perfect child," in light of man's inhumanity to man as individually and collectively acted out across the span of millennia?

How could 2000 years of biblical preparation and prophecy point not toward Jesus of Nazareth but another 1800 years _beyond_ him to Mrs. Eddy of Boston? How could all the civilizing accomplishments of Christendom from Constantine to Lincoln have been founded upon a mistake? Far-fetched indeed.

Then consider _eternity_. The word, the concept, was familiar enough to me from Eddy's textbook, but I had never thoughtfully applied it to myself. Who and what, exactly, did I expect to be after my short span on this earth was over, time was done away with, and eternal life was now mine for the living, world without end?

Christian Science metaphysics told me I'd be an idea, a concept, a bundle of spiritual qualities — gloriously so, to be sure — but it all sounded like a dull comedown from everyday life here on our beautiful planet, my life as a person wonderfully (for the most part, anyway) interwoven with countless other persons, all sparkling with interest and variety, no two the same. Impersonality couldn't begin to compare.

That in turn brought up _heaven_ and _hell_. Jesus, the Master Christian as we were taught to call him, had a lot to say about both, the one almost unimaginably joyous and loving and lovely, the other almost unimaginably agonizing and awful.

Why then did Christian Science reduce hell to nothing but an erroneous mental condition and heaven to (as I described above) uninviting, undifferentiated, impersonal perfection? The one scarcely to be feared, the other not particularly to be desired.

If I wanted heaven as a kingdom of splendor, an Eden restored, a New Jerusalem shining—heaven as in every way grander, not blander, than earthly experience—*Science and Health* wasn't the book for me. The Bible was.

Likewise if some of the hellish scenes of St. John's Revelation were in fact a revelation and not just a bad dream, I'd better get serious about washing in the blood of the Lamb, Mrs. Eddy to the contrary notwithstanding.

No Way Out

What I think began to happen, looking back on it, was that from my baseline of already taking God and the Bible, the church and the sin problem, quite seriously, some beneficially disruptive events in my life caused me to start taking my metaphysically smug self <u>less</u> seriously and those other issues of history and eternity, heaven and hell, <u>more</u> seriously.

A life-altering spiral, a paradigm shift, a series of falling dominoes, then ensued which led to my suddenly beholding in the mirror one day the man I actually was—words terribly difficult to say but finally impossible not to say—a sinner in need of a Savior.

Jesus Christ rocked my world. Christian Science had "taken away my Lord," taken from me even the reverence to call him by that ancient royal title, and laid him I knew not where (John 20:13). Now, seemingly overnight (though really it was years in the making), I had discovered him and realized he is the key to everything.

Jesus too was a someone, or a something, that I had noddingly taken notice of but never taken seriously enough, never at all. I knew all *about* him, a head-knowledge I could glibly verbalize by the hour, without ever actually *knowing* him for real. (Exactly the tragic disconnect the Lord warns of in Matthew 7:23.)

Now at last, that person-to-person connection swept over me and swept me away. The reason this could finally occur as it did, I believe, is that by my already having taken God, the Bible, the church, and the sin problem quite seriously while remaining, as best I knew, a committed Christian Scientist, those four factors began to close in me from all sides when friends urged me to take Jesus seriously. I saw no way out.

Soon enough then, though not without a struggle, I gave my life to him and began the slow process of disentangling my life from the Mary Baker Eddy teachings.

A Template?

That's the way it went for one young sold-out Christian Scientist thirty to forty years ago. The question now is how much of a template one can draw from my conversion experience for a dialogue with Christian Scientists who we're hoping will consider the claims of Christ.

Call them Greg and Kim. Can his seriousness about God and the church, her seriousness about the Bible and self-examination — that is, the sin problem by another name — become starting points for the evangelism we seek to initiate with them?

Might we get somewhere by saying, "Look, Greg, what if the God you so love really did incarnate himself as Jesus in the virgin's womb?"

Or, "Wait, Kim, aren't we cutting the heart out of the Bible, both testaments, if we don't admit the whole thing is about Jesus, Genesis to Revelation?"

Such were the sort of appeals, grounded in what I already took seriously, that more and more powerfully worked upon me until I was at last irresistibly persuaded of the gospel and thus dissuaded (partly at first, and later completely) from Mrs. Eddy's spell.

And they might work similarly with a Kim or a Greg — provided the CSer had already been put off balance by what I've called the beneficially disruptive life events that can make yesterday's know-it-all metaphysician into today's almost-humble seeker of true truth.

Exploration, experimentation, and experience alone will tell. I think it is certainly worth investigating. The self-enforcing circularity of Eddyism isn't unbreakable, after all, or you and I would never have managed to break out of it. We serve a waters-parting, mountain-moving God: to him be the glory.

Published in May 2020
on the Ananias website

SHOPPING FOR A HOME

Imagine you're sitting in a coffee shop, somewhere near the Christian Science headquarters in Boston or the Principia campus in St. Louis, and one of the voices at the table behind you mentions Science. Over the next few minutes you can't help overhearing the following conversation among three individuals who evidently once followed Mrs. Eddy but are no longer doing so.

Timothy: I'm interested to meet another couple who decided, like my wife and me, Christian Science was not for them after having both been raised in it and having had it in their families for generations. What brought you to that point?

Priscilla: The healing promises of Christian Science were just not fulfilled in my experience and in our children's experience. And the church was not the loving place you'd expect from all their talk of "God is Love." So much denial, impersonality, and pretense; so little genuine warmth or acceptance or simple caring.

Aquila: For me, it was a matter of theology, history, and evidence. I concluded *Science and Health* was just not true to the Bible, especially in terms of who Jesus was. How could Mrs. Eddy throw over what the Christian church had been for over 1800 years? How could I live by her metaphysical statements that "man is not material" (Scientific Statement of Being, SH 468:15) or "sin and evil are unreal" (the Tenets, SH 497:9) when real life proved otherwise?

Timothy: As former Christian Scientists, where have you landed spiritually now?

Aquila: Nowhere in particular, I'm afraid. We've gone to church occasionally, here and there. But they're all so different from what we're used to, and really so different from each other. Amid all their disagreements, who's to say what's true? I've almost decided, why bother?

Priscilla: We still believe in God, of course. We pray and rely on Him. We want to live good lives as He would have us live, and I think we do.

Timothy: What exactly is God to you, though, if He is no longer Mrs. Eddy's seven synonyms? And what's it mean to live as He would have us live? How can we know that?

Priscilla: Oh, straight from the Bible, wouldn't you say, AQ? Don't misunderstand, Tim. It's still very important to us. The Ten Commandments, the Sermon on the Mount, some of the Psalms, the love chapter in Corinthians, the fruits of the Spirit that Paul writes about.

Aquila: I love where Jesus says, "The kingdom of God is within you" (Luke 17:21). We live by that. And actually the synonyms still define God pretty well for me. Principle, for example. And divine Mind, the all-knowing. Life, Truth, Love — we didn't leave those when we left the CS church.

Timothy: Aquila, let me go back to what you said about *Science and Health* misrepresenting the biblical Jesus. How was that?

Aquila: Jesus' disciples and all the New Testament writers believed him to be God in the flesh. They expected his second coming. They worshiped him in the Eucharist of bread and wine. Mrs. Eddy denies all of that and yet claims to provide the "final revelation" of Christianity (SH 107:5). The contradictions became so troubling to me, I just walked away from all of it.

Timothy: I wrestled with those same contradictions, but the conclusion I reached was to stop following Mrs. Eddy and follow Jesus. Put *Science and Health* aside and believe the Bible.

Priscilla: When you've been taught for so long to approach religion scientifically and not from blind faith — studied and worked at it so hard — and the whole scientific thing sort of collapses, that childlike attitude of "follow Jesus, believe the Bible" is hard to recover. My CS teacher called it old theology. I respected her so much. I still do.

Aquila: As I said, Tim, evidence is important to me. Facts and logic. Simply deciding to believe something seems arbitrary, almost superstitious.

Timothy: I respect that. We have to be tough-minded. There are a lot of myths and superstitions out there. But when you think about it, we all believe a lot of things axiomatically or by inference, rather than by direct proof. Physicists admit they can't explain gravity. Yet we all take it for granted, because it literally is granted. It's just there. I take God at His word because no better alternative has ever been presented. What keeps you from doing that? Can you put your finger on it?

Aquila: No offense, but it's just too simplistic for me. I couldn't respect myself. Sorry.

Priscilla: I guess I'm the same. Old theology, formulas, pat answers. The blood of the Lamb, believe and be saved — the world has moved beyond all that. We're educated people. It's the 21st century.

Timothy: Look, you said God and the Bible are important to you, right?

Both: Right.

Timothy: Well, then we come to the hard part. I think you need to honestly ask yourselves, how important are they? Am I taking them on my terms, picking and choosing? Or am I willing to really submit to them on their terms? That's a scary word, isn't it? "Submit!"

Priscilla: Uncomfortable is how I'd put it. And a little demeaning, you know. It goes against the grain for a modern woman.

Timothy: I said this part is hard. Pushing ahead when something is uncomfortable or demeaning, what does that take, AQ?

Aquila: Obviously courage on one hand, and on the other hand, a degree of humility. But not so fast, Tim. You're setting it up as though someone who does otherwise is a lesser person. That feels manipulative.

Timothy: Please don't take it that way. I'm just trying to show you there's more than one way of seeing it. AQ wondered if he could respect himself for submitting to God's word, as some of us have. But maybe I couldn't respect myself if I didn't.

Priscilla: I suppose it would be easier to have one authority for everything, one source for the answer to all questions. Not have to think things out for yourself and have big areas of uncertainty. Recite the creed and that's that.

Timothy: Easier or harder? A minute ago my way was distasteful to you, uncomfortable. As far as creeds are concerned, they're not some kind of mumbo jumbo. A creed is just a clear, specific summation of what you hold to be true. Everybody has one, but with most people they're unconscious, implicit. I'd rather have mine explicit and on the table.

Aquila: Fair enough. I'm with you there.

Timothy: As you probably recall, rejection of creeds is taught by Mrs. Eddy in her textbook and mentioned in her hymns. It's right there in her *Church Manual*, where she speaks of forming "a church without creeds" (17:3). So it was a group of people joining together to serve God but not binding themselves to a definitive statement of who God is and how He relates to us. How was that supposed to work? No wonder the CS church has drifted and declined. In the terms of Jesus' parable, it's a sand-built house (Matthew 7:24-27).

Priscilla: Really sad. So many good, faithful people. Such earnest good intentions. Noble institutions like Principia and Adventure Unlimited. A hundred years in my own family. But you're right, Tim. It's built on sand.

Timothy: How about the two of you, now that Science is a closed chapter? What are you building on?

Priscilla: I don't see that we really have to. We're just going along, doing the best we can. Being there for our kids, working at our careers, contributing in our community. That's enough, wouldn't you say, AQ? Sometimes more than enough, as busy as we are, as hectic as things get. But at least without that heavy, restrictive pressure to conform and measure up that we felt in Christian Science.

Aquila: Yes, hon, it's a relief to be out from under that. But I can see Tim's point. Everybody has to have a core of conviction, a fundamental sense of what's real, what's important. How the world works. The jumbled wishful made-up picture that CS gives was part of what we walked away from, after all. What do we have now in its place?

Timothy: Thank you both for being patient and hanging with me in this discussion. I think we're getting somewhere. Come back to that image of the two houses, one built on sand, unsafe to live in, the other built on rock. Jesus said the rock was his own teachings and example—actually his own person, himself. Remember that?

Aquila: Sure, we learned it in Sunday School when I was six. Mrs. Line. I can still see her face.

Timothy: AQ, you mentioned all the disagreement among Christian churches and denominations, causing you to throw up your hands. I get that. But after leaving Science, doing a lot of study and searching, looking around, I found there is more agreement than disagreement among them. For instance, the Apostles' Creed. It's a few simple points about what's true and real, that all of Jesus' followers have accepted for over a thousand years, and still do. Here's a sheet I printed off the Web. As you see, there are only a dozen short lines, a hundred words. You can say them in less than a minute. For a thoughtful person like either of you, probably the hardest ones to say are the first two, "I believe."[21]

Priscilla: You mean because we won't just do it by rote? It has to be from the whole heart?

Aquila: And the whole mind.

Timothy: Yes, nothing less is good enough. Not for ourselves, and actually not for God either. When we say, "I believe in God the Father, Almighty, Maker of heaven and earth," He doesn't want it to come from parrots or puppets. He wants that intelligent submission I was talking about, clear-thinking persons with their eyes wide open, looking up to Him of their own free will. There doesn't have to be utter certainty. How can there be? We're human. So maybe we're really saying I believe that I believe, or I'm trying to believe, or I want to believe. But we're taking that plunge.

Priscilla: Like the man who said to Jesus, "I believe. Help thou mine unbelief" (Mark 9:24).

Timothy: Exactly. So here we are up on the high dive. Want to plunge, AQ? How about it? Do you believe in God the Father, Almighty, Maker of heaven and earth?

Aquila: I guess I do, yes. It's hard to spit out, but the alternative, the denial or disbelief of Him, is much worse. Even the cowardice of saying I don't know is worse.

Priscilla: I believe too.

Aquila: So have we just plunged?

Timothy: That's for you to answer, friends, not me.

Priscilla: It feels like we have.

Timothy: Before we look at the next few lines, let me point out a couple of things that make the creed different from the sort of propositions and assertions we grew up on as Christian Scientists. One, it uses words of plain meaning, not the abstract, rarefied terminology that Mrs. Eddy uses. "Maker of heaven and earth" is

---

[21] See full text of the Apostles' Creed in Appendix B

pretty straightforward, right? Nothing about mortal mind or divine ideas or anything like that. Accept it or reject it. Common sense suffices. Second, unlike the CS picture of things in a sort of diagram, a static layout of "the way it is," the creed moves like a sort of story — things that have happened, and that will happen, and the persons involved in those happenings.

Aquila: That's logical enough. Anyone's life is a story. So is any given day, for that matter. So is the Bible itself.

Timothy: Also you'll notice that the persons in the creed, beginning with the Father, Son, and Holy Ghost, are part of its common-sense realism. Again, words of plain meaning. The way that CS impersonalized everything and everybody, ourselves included, had come to seem so fake to me. Whereas this is something you can take hold of and hang onto, even if the theological depth of it takes longer to fathom. I sure haven't fathomed it yet. But it's a rock to build on.

Priscilla: Interesting, yes. That was part of my CS exit too. By introspection and just by looking in the mirror, it's obvious I'm a human person. And married to one. But, God as a person? That's not obvious. On the other hand, the complexity and interest and even beauty that we see in human persons, if God didn't possess that in even higher degree, if He were just an impersonal principle, He would be to that extent less than we are — which is totally upside down. But back to the creed, Tim. How does the next part go?

Timothy: All right, now listen to how the storyline picks up, the interplay of the persons. Not forces, persons. "I believe in God the Father, Almighty, Maker of heaven and earth. And in Jesus Christ, His only begotten Son, our Lord, who was conceived by the Holy Ghost, born of the Virgin Mary, suffered under Pontius Pilate, was crucified, dead, and buried." It goes on, but let's pause there. That's already a lot to take in. Billions of people around the world bend the knee and subscribe to this. A few hundred thousand of Mrs. Eddy's followers do not.

Aquila: It doesn't actually say Jesus was God, or is God, does it? I always thought that was explicit in the Apostles' Creed. That's something I really stumble on.

Timothy: You were taught to. We all were. But it's certainly implicit when the creed says "only begotten Son." As humans, when we have a son, he's human. Not fish or fowl. Not conceptual, either. Not just an idea. So when God has a Son, capital S, it's no different. It's the original of all sonship, in fact. Jesus came first, before we or any son of ours was ever thought of, before there was time. Christian Science talks about sonship, of course, but as I said, it dances around the plain meaning of who and what Jesus the Son had to be if he was begotten of God the Father. He had to be God as well, God the Son.

Priscilla: Why does that matter so much, Tim?

Timothy: I could flip the question around and ask you, why do Mrs. Eddy and those who buy into her view of things resist it so much? Maybe because of its implications for how big and sovereign God would have to be, if the creed is right, and in consequence how small and utterly dependent we'd have to be. We want a manageable God who fits into our logic, our box. It gives us a sense of mastery and control to be able to say God couldn't become flesh and be born of Mary and live and die as Jesus. Nor could Jesus be fully God and fully man at the same time. "He just couldn't," we say. "I reject that." Notice how big the "I" is in that statement. How small God is. It's grotesque. One day all this dawned on me, and I was horrified at the arrogance. Who did I think I was?

Aquila: It's unpleasant to think I've indulged that kind of arrogance. You're getting to me, Tim. But obviously the creed doesn't stop there. The resurrection still has to occur. Tell us the rest.

Timothy: Okay, we paused where Jesus was in the tomb, right? So it continues this way: "He descended into hell. The third day he rose again from the dead. He ascended into heaven, and sits at the right hand of God the Father Almighty. From thence he shall come to judge the quick and the dead."

Priscilla: Stop again, please. Let me see if I'm following this. It's saying heaven and hell are real places, not just a state of mind. It speaks of Jesus in the present tense, sitting at God's right hand. Even now at this moment. It has him coming back, and when he comes, judging everyone, me included. Do I have that right, and if so, what's to be the judgment upon me? That has an uncomfortable note of finality.

Timothy: It does, and that's why the creed itself matters. What we believe matters. Committing ourselves to Jesus puts us within his embrace as the Savior before we ever have to face his tribunal as the Judge. It gets us forgiven, made new by the indwelling of his own Spirit, and adopted into his family of sanctified ones, or saints. All of which in fact paraphrases the closing lines of the creed that I'll come to now. First, though, tell me how you're doing. I hope I haven't lost you, buried you with too much too fast.

Aquila: I think I'm tracking you pretty well. The initial "I believe" is what has to hold up through each clause of the story and each claim about who Jesus was and is. If I can set aside my doubt and sophistication—actually amounting to arrogance, as you pointed out—enough to accept this person called God the Son and Jesus the man, both one and the same, all the rest of it isn't that hard to accept either. Of course the whole thing for me at this point is still just a thought experiment, totally provisional. But I'm not ruling it out as I would have yesterday. Honey?

Priscilla: That's about where I am too, at this point, Tim. I have to admit it stirs me. It pulls on me. I'm really touched that you'd be so patient with both of us about this. You have your convictions, and you hold them passionately, I can tell. But you aren't pushing them on us.

Timothy: There was a time when I was exactly where both of you are. It's so sad when someone who has given up on Christian Science then gives up on God and Jesus and the Bible as well. It doesn't need to be, but it happens so often. What's left for them to build on then? Sand. Shifting, slippery, squishy, seductive, unstable, treacherous sand. If I can help you see a better way, *the* better way, I want to.

Priscilla: You paraphrased the ending, but walk us through the exact words.

Timothy: The closing lines come back and repeat our affirmation of belief, actually twice: "I believe in the Holy Ghost. I believe in the holy catholic church; the communion of saints; the forgiveness of sins; the resurrection of the body; and the life everlasting. Amen."

Aquila: Communion of saints? Catholic church? Help me out.

Timothy: That's "catholic" with a small C. It just means one universal church, permanent, enduring, and undivided — in God's sight, anyway, and in our aspiration, our faith, even though it's terribly divided in the here and now — and often terribly unholy. The communion of saints is a related idea. To me it means that everyone who ever has made or ever will make this affirmation of belief is bonded together in the family of God — the saved and sanctified ones, the saints — across all space and time. I find that a beautiful picture, don't you? It grounds me in a way Mrs. Eddy's metaphysics never did.

Priscilla: Beautiful, yes. It does have a lot of appeal. And as for grounding, something just made me think of that line in one of Mrs. Eddy's hymns: "Thus Truth engrounds me on the rock, upon Life's shore" (*Christian Science Hymnal*, No. 253).

Aquila: "'Gainst which the winds and waves can shock, oh, nevermore." Some rock, as far as Pris and I were concerned. Some shore. Real life eventually washed us back out to sea.

Timothy: I'd have to say that's because it was never more than a sandbar in the first place. Mrs. Eddy and the Christian Scientists are a strange case. They talk so reverently about Jesus, yet they're afraid of him and the claims he made about himself. Their Jesus isn't the divine man of the creed, God's only begotten Son, our Lord, who is alive now at the Father's right hand and who is coming back in judgment. She describes him as simply "the highest human concept" (SH 482:19). You said it: not much of a rock to stand the storms. CS just seems to want to play with words that sound nice but don't connect to anything. That hymn Pris quoted, for example, is called "Christ My Refuge." It talks about kissing the cross and wanting to be "nearer Thee, where Thine own children are." But at the end of the day, so what? Everything is metaphysicalized to the vanishing point. Jesus the King of Kings, the Lion and the Lamb, crucified and risen, reigning now and returning soon, is nowhere to be found.

Aquila: So we built on a supposed rock that was no rock, all three of us and so many others who bought into the Mary Baker Eddy dream. But just because one rock was false, it doesn't mean there is no true rock.

Priscilla: I think we made that assumption after leaving CS just because we had been so burned. We were so turned off.

Aquila: And maybe kind of giddy, just to be out from under all the guilt and denial and double-talk. The freedom was heady. But that's worn off. Now we both feel kind of adrift, honestly.

Timothy: Jesus didn't say building on sand is impossible. He said it's unreliable, insecure, unsatisfying. It doesn't last. Eventually comes disillusionment, then distress, then disaster. He invites us, and frankly, he warns us, to build on him — on his own person, his promises, his saving sacrifice and victory on our behalf. So thanks for the talk. Think about it. Think hard. Where do you want to build? As I asked you before, if not on this rock, where?

Published in August 2014
on the Ananias website

A FATHER WHO COMES RUNNING

Our friend Sandra is a very devout Christian Scientist, gradually getting into the public practice. We've noticed that sometimes, along with her metaphysical vocabulary, she uses a more biblical or traditional phrasing about "trusting the Father" or "listening to the Father," that kind of thing. Then it's back to Mrs. Eddy's synonyms for God—Principle, Mind, Soul, etc.

When the time is right, I want to ask her how God can be both of those things, divine Principle on the one hand and yet our Father on the other hand. Recently as I studied Jesus' parable of the Prodigal Son in Luke 15:11-32, it struck me how inescapably personal that father and both his sons are.

I'd like to challenge Sandra to account in Christian Science metaphysical terms for everything this father, as Jesus portrays him, does. He first gives both his sons life in body and soul, gives them a living to sustain them, and gives them free will to love and obey him in return, or not.

Then the father lets his younger son run away and disgrace himself, Yet he never stops watching for the boy to return, and finally seeing him do so, runs to meet him more than halfway, then waves off the boy's apology and lavishes him with undeserved grace.

Next he is equally as patient with the older brother's self-righteousness as he was with the younger brother's self-indulgence. The father again goes beyond expectations to reconcile the sinfully selfish firstborn to himself.

Though well aware of each son's flaws, he is kindly, merciful, and generous to both—even as they are grasping, unloving, and ungrateful to him and to each other.

So I just want to ask Sandra how in the world this portrayal of the wise, forgiving father and the woefully wayward children can possibly be squared with the impersonal "perfect God and perfect man" she reads about in *Science and Health* (259:13).

And I'd ask her as well: Who wouldn't want a wonderful, understanding Father like this, a Father God who gave his only begotten Son, instead of a cold impersonal divine Principle?

You can't have both, dear Sandy. Choose ye this day!

Published in November 2019
on the Ananias website

"*O come, let us adore him, Christ the Lord*" (Dore)

CHAPTER 8:
WHAT BETTER PLACE TO TAKE MY STAND?

Increasingly, biblical Christianity felt to me like a better fit with everyday realities than Christian Science. Its pulsing heartbeat answered to my experience, my common sense, and my inmost hunger in a way Mrs. Eddy's cold metaphysics never did. I had a joyous feeling of coming home. Never too late to begin anew.

NOT BY CHANCE

My dad loved to quote a church signboard he once saw: "Be careful what you say and do. You may be someone's only contact with the Bible." I saw the force of that with new clarity when our campus pastor at Colorado Christian University, where I was then working, challenged a group of us to think in depth about how we first came to know the Lord.

The events of a week in July 1980, when my lifelong identification as a follower of Mrs. Eddy was rocked to its foundations by the irresistible claims of Jesus Christ, are a story I have told countless times (most recently in Chapter 1 of this book), and thanked God for again and again.

But it was only when going over those events prayerfully and anew, at the pastor's urging, that I realized for the very first time how it had been one college freshman, seemingly a bit player in the drama, who was in fact the vital link that connected the whole chain God used to reach me.

Laurie, I think her name was. She was on a summer evangelism trip to Boulder with the Intervarsity group she had joined at Stanford after breaking with her Christian Science upbringing. Annie, her younger sister, was at the Adventure Unlimited camp in Buena Vista (for which I happened to work) that same week.

Plot Twist

Their mother asked me to contact Laurie and take her to visit Annie, hoping this would pull the older sister back toward Science. The plot twist, which I won't relate in detail here, was that I ended up being the one pulled — into the gospel embrace of a Savior who has held me ever after.

What I never fully realized until now was this: absent the hungry, humble, bold, brave turn toward the Christ of Scripture by this girl not yet 20, my opportunity to make that same turn as an accomplished, admired, self-important professional man of almost 40 would not have come about. Laurie led the way, and the Father scripted the whole improbable sequence!

I marvel at it. She was like the "little maid," nameless in II Kings 5:2, working as a house slave in Syria after being abducted from her people in Israel, who spoke up fearlessly to tell the great Naaman, her leprous master, of the living God who could heal him.

Or like the "lad here" in John 6:9, who dared get close enough to Jesus' men that his few bits of fish and bread could be used to feed thousands. Or like the "little child" in Matthew 18:2 who was in the right place at the right time to serve as the Lord's example of who is fit for the Kingdom. Like all of these, young Laurie the humble seeker after eternal life blazed a trail to the foot of the Cross for proud confident John.

I only talked to her for a few minutes a few times, and she never really witnessed to me; at least not in words. I don't know her last name, or where she is now, and I wouldn't recognize her if we met again. I don't even know if she has remained a follower of Jesus. But I have remained so, most gratefully. What this little maid "up and did" was all the witness I needed, just at that unexpectedly dramatic moment in my life.

Sifting back through the whole experience lately has filled me with awe and gratitude at God's grace as never before, and made me all the more determined to witness at every chance (aloud or silently) through the Ananias website and every other channel open to me, for those who may be helped onward to Him—even if I never know it.

Laurie surely never knew the part she played in my conversion. Yet our encounter was not by chance. How wisely and truly it has been said: "Be careful what you say and do. You may be someone's only contact with the Bible."

Published in February 2012
on the Ananias website

MY DOORWAY OUT

"Behold, what *manner* of love." These words from the Epistle of John are etched on the memory of anyone who spent years attending the Christian Science church.

They begin the I John 3:1-3 passage that Mary Baker Eddy directed to be read at the close of every Sunday service as the supposed correlative Scripture (*Manual* 121) to her pantheistic, gnostical, matter-denying formula, the purported Scientific Statement of Being (SH 468).

By God's providence, however (or might we say by God's sense of humor) this very passage came to play a crucial part in my dawning awareness that biblical truth must stand above and apart from any of Eddy's theories. Which then eventually led to my escape from Christian Science and my salvation by Jesus Christ.

It happened this way. Throughout the 1980s after my initial surrender to Christ's Lordship, I flailed around trying to have one foot in the Gospel and the other in my Christian Science upbringing. My custom then (as now) was to pray aloud each morning the Lord's Prayer and a series of other petitions and affirmations. One of those was I John 3:1-3, given in the King James Bible as follows:

> (1) Behold, what manner of love the Father hath bestowed upon us, that we should be called the sons of God: therefore the world knoweth us not, because it knew him not. (2) Beloved, now are we the sons of God, and it doth not yet appear what we shall be: but we know that, when he shall appear, we shall be like him; for we shall see him as he is. (3) And every man that hath this hope in him purifieth himself, even as he is pure.

Dividing my Sundays—even as my heart was still divided—between attending Christian Science services and worshiping hungrily at various nearby Protestant churches, I found myself wanting "more of Jesus" in those weekday devotional times. "God in Three Persons, Blessed Trinity," as the Doxology calls Him, increasingly dominated my thoughts, overruling the Mrs. Eddy abstraction of "infinite Mind and its infinite manifestation" (SH 468:10).

We'll Be Like Jesus

So one day it occurred to me that the kind of love God loves us with would be better illumined by inviting the Trinity into that I John passage where each of the "he" and "him" pronouns appears in King James. I tried it, and the result was this:

> (1) Behold, what manner of love the Father hath bestowed upon us, that we should be called the sons of God: therefore the world knoweth us not, because it knew not *Jesus Christ.* (2) Beloved, now are we the sons of God, and it doth not yet appear what we shall be: but we know that, when *Jesus* shall appear, we shall be like him; for we shall see *the Son as the Father* is. (3) And every man that hath this hope in *Jesus Christ* purifieth himself, even as *the Father, Son, and Holy Ghost* is pure.

By substituting these few words, we see into the passage clarity. The text is not a cold metaphysical *diagram* as Mrs. Eddy tried to make it. Rather it is a compelling salvation *story* with beginning, middle, and end. Walk through it with me:

We see the story moving swiftly from the pathos of our failing to recognize Jesus when he came among us, resulting in the Cross—to the hope we now have in his return and the purification we experience in awaiting that.

We then see it moving to the encouragement to persevere as pilgrims and strangers in a world uncomprehending of Christ and his followers, and finally to the glorious anticipation of his fleshly reappearing and our at last becoming exactly like him—adopted brothers and sisters to the risen, ascended, and reigning Lord.

Praying this aloud day by day, I came into a clearer, surer knowledge of myself as Jesus' own disciple and sheep, not as Mrs. Eddy self-rescuing student. Through trinitarian prayer, her misapplied correlative Scripture" became my doorway out of Christian Science darkness into Christ's redeeming light and love.

Published in September 2019
on the Ananias website

UNDONE

Christmas is beloved to me as a season of new birth personally, as well as a celebration of Jesus' birth. Over the years as a young adult Christian Scientist, raising our kids, teaching Sunday school, active with Adventure Unlimited and Principia, I found that those expectant weeks in December were filling me not only with joyous anticipation but also with tense disquiet.

That's because it had become harder and harder for my wife and me to reconcile Mrs. Eddy's cool diminishing of Jesus with the "Come let us adore Him" warmth of Christmastime. We began to have a similar struggle around Easter each year.

Somehow this gave me permission to dig deeper into Scripture, to hungrily visit the Christmas and Easter services at Christian churches, and to question more searchingly the whole framework of Christian theology.

Christmas undid me—that's the best way I can put it. Our Lord Jesus, the Hound of Heaven as he has been called, used those sacred times of year when "the manger and the cross tell their story" (an Eddy phrase, interestingly, SH 142:15) to corner and capture me to himself at last.

In keeping with the custom of suggesting books for Christmas reading or giving, I offer the following gift list of titles that had particular impact for my own coming to the Cross, during those momentous years from the late 1970s to the early 1990s.

The Everlasting Man — G. K. Chesterton
Mere Christianity — C. S. Lewis
Unspoken Sermons — George MacDonald
Your God Is Too Small — J. B. Phillips
Apologia Pro Vita Sua — John Henry Newman
Jesus Rediscovered — Malcolm Muggeridge
Who Is Jesus? — R. C. Sproul
More Than a Carpenter — Josh McDowell

The gospel treasure these writers offer is the best present you could give yourself, whether at Advent season or any time of year. I guarantee it, wishing a holy and merry Christmas to you and yours. "God bless us, every one!"

Published in December 2009
on the Ananias website

BORN TO ADORE

"I was free born." With these words in Acts 22:28, the Apostle Paul is not stating a spiritual truth, not at all. He is making a purely political point. The context has him comparing notes with the centurion, a naturalized Roman, on how the two obtained their citizenship.

Mary Baker Eddy's use of his statement as if it proves something theologically or ontologically (SH 227:17) is very revealing.

Her incomprehension of how utterly lost mankind are, her deval-uation of Jesus' saving work, and her unreliability as a biblical interpreter are nowhere better illustrated than by this howling misquotation—and by the extended discussion of freedom and slavery in which it occurs, on pages 224-228 of *Science and Health*.

In this brief essay I won't attempt to analyze those five pages line by line, though it's a project worth your time for anyone wish-ing to put Christian Science to the test. The overall thrust is that slavery or bondage or oppression is of our own making, a product of false belief—"because some public teachers permit an ignorance of divine power" (227:10)—and that freedom or liberty or domin-ion is therefore within reach if mortals will just accept Mrs. Eddy's portrayal of things and "assert their [in-born] freedom in the name of Almighty God" (228:14).

She makes analogies to the abolition of slavery in the United States and to the Hebrew exodus from Egypt, casting herself by implication as another Lincoln or even another Moses. She repeat-edly invokes "the rights of man," a concept beloved of Americans but unknown in Scripture. She does not mention Jesus except briefly near the end of the passage, pages 227 and 228, and then only as a teacher and exemplar, not as the Savior by whom alone our bondage to sin is broken.

"Truth makes man free," she says at 225:3, paraphrasing Jesus' promise in John 8:32. But the metaphysical abstraction just floats there (as it does on the walls of Christian Science churches), unteth-ered from Jesus' warning in succeeding verses that we're all slaves until the Son himself personally liberates us.

Whereas Paul well understood this doctrine of man's hopeless bondage and Christ's gracious redemption, as he makes clear in such passages as Romans 7-8, Galatians 4-5, and Colossians 1-4.

What Paul Knew

Even when born again and specially commissioned as an apostle, Roman citizenship and all its rights notwithstanding, Paul continued to struggle with the sinner's unfreedom, a predicament he couldn't think himself out of. "With the mind I myself serve the law of God; but with the flesh the law of sin" (Romans 7:25). Only in Christ Jesus was he made free from that servitude (Romans 8:2) and liberated from the carnal mind with its living death, its enmity against God (Romans 8: 6,7).

Contrast Mrs. Eddy's lofty but empty platitude, bloodless and ultimately powerless, "Love is the liberator" (SH 225:21), with Paul's tough-minded emancipation proclamation in Colossians, explaining how the Son has "delivered [freed] us from the power of darkness" with "redemption [ransom, the slave-price] through his blood" (Colossians 1:13-14).

The gnostic heresy of self-salvation, confronted in Colossians only to reappear eons later in Christian Science, is refuted with Paul's reminder that the cancellation of "ordinances against us [our slave papers]" required not just an assertion but a transaction, the sacrificial death and victory of Jesus, who "nail[ed] it to his cross… spoiled [the enslaving] powers…and triumph[ed] over them" (Colossians 2:14,15).

"The enslavement of man is not legitimate," insists *Science and Health* (228:11). With that we can agree. But it is not imaginary either. It is a fact, the very real consequence of the Fall, humanity's rebellion against God. Since everyone is thereby enslaved, attempting to think our way free, the Eddy approach, doesn't work. We need a Savior to *set* us free, and we have him in Jesus Christ.

For all the freedom-talk of my fifty years in Christian Science, I remained shackled to my own fallen and sinning self, "the old man" (Colossians 3:9). Only when I came to know and trust the God who died for me, rose for me, reigns for me, intercedes for me, and will return for me, did I really come to know "the glorious liberty of the children of God" (Romans 8:21, quoted out of context at SH 227:24).

As mentioned, we Americans are powerfully stirred by the idea of liberty as a birthright. So it may seem odd to find C. S. Lewis saying the opposite: "I was not born to be free. I was born to adore and obey."[22] This clashes with our proud sense of freeborn self-hood. Yet I'd have to say it matches my experience.

My adoring and obedient submission to the Lord Jesus became the doorway to whatever spiritual freedom I now enjoy — and that freedom is not the license to do as I please, rather it is but the capability and commitment to do what pleases my God: Father, Son, and Holy Spirit.

Published in September 2014
on the Ananias website

IN PLAIN SIGHT

Up to my mid-thirties I was a Christian Scientist following Mary Baker Eddy instead of Jesus.

Then for a dozen years I was a Christian Scientist trying to follow Jesus and Mrs. Eddy both.

Finally things reached a breaking point, and I became a born-again Christian following Jesus Christ alone. The warning in I John 4:1, "Try the spirits," played a decisive part.

This thought and others from that same rich chapter were familiar to me from long study of the *Christian Science Quarterly* Bible lessons. But I knew them only as fragmentary platitudes, not in their context.

"God is Love" (I John 4:8), said the lettering on the church walls. But where was the proof? "Perfect love casts out fear" (I John

[22] As spoken to his friend A.C. Harwood, cited in *C.S. Lewis at the Breakfast Table*, edited by James Como

4:18), said the periodicals. But what fear in particular, and whose love was anywhere near perfect?

Although the answers were right there on the page, I couldn't see them. *Science and Health*, purporting to be the key to the Scriptures, functioned for me more like a lock. The Word was not laid open but shut away, its intended meaning, key themes, and central persons—Jesus in particular—all hiding in plain sight.

So long as I deferred to Mrs. Eddy's interpretation of the text, important passages in the Bible were closed to me, and the plain meaning of other passages was overwritten with her own invented meaning. Sensing this, I struggled against it for years. At last I could defer to Mrs. Eddy no longer.

From now on I would read *Science and Health* in terms of the Bible, not the Bible in terms of *Science and Health*. The textbook would remain for me a helpful commentary (as I then thought but now no longer think), but never again an authority. Scripture must be uppermost.

The proof that God is Love, long hidden from me in plain sight, was now manifest. It was "that God has sent His only begotten Son into the world so that we might live through Him" (I John 4:9). The missing piece was Jesus.

More to Learn

I still had more to learn—and unlearn. After blowing up my marriage with selfishness and sensuality (and while First Reader in my branch church), it was not God's perfect child that I saw in the mirror, but a monster of sin and shame.

The fear of hell in eternity, and of a living hell as a failed husband and father, shook me to the core. That Savior who had never meant much to me? Suddenly I needed him like a drowning man.

Again my answered prayers jumped off the page. A Father who personally loved us had "sent His son to be the propitiation," or blood sacrifice, for my sins (I John 4:10). It was by confessing Jesus that His love would be perfected in me, so I might "have confidence in the day of judgment," all fear of hell cast out (I John 4:17).

Unlearning in this desperate hour my self-delusion of sinless identity as taught in *Science and Health* (see page 290:25, among others), I was able to reconcile with my family and begin anew as a self-styled "Christian Scientist for Jesus."

For over a decade I reveled in growing closer to Jesus, finding his footprints throughout Mrs. Eddy's writings, and trying to witness about him to fellow Scientists.

But more and more I realized that the heresy C.S. Lewis calls "Christianity and" — the vain effort to improve on Jesus' saving work — was holding me back from the Kingdom. (See *The Screwtape Letters*, Chapter 25.)

Why continue to trust a teaching that had kept my Lord and Savior hidden for so long? Didn't the refusal of *Science and Health* to confess "that Jesus is come in the flesh" as God incarnate (see page 361:2, among others), reflect "the spirit of the antichrist" (I John 4:3-4)? Didn't this identify the book's author with those "false prophets" of whom I John 4:1 warns?

Obeying the Apostle John's command to "Try the spirits," I had no choice but to become Jesus' man entirely and exclusively. I had found the missing piece, the God-man hidden in plain sight. I was home at last.

Published in July 2015
on the Ananias website

"The Lord is my shepherd; I shall not want" (Psalm 23:1).

CHAPTER 9:
HOW CAN I EVER THANK HIM ENOUGH?

Looking back over all the forgiveness I've received from God and God's people, all the wrong turns I've made along life's road, all the beauty and delight I've experienced in confessing myself a sinner saved by the grace of Jesus Christ, set free and at the same time bonded to him, I never tire of telling that old story, singing that new song.

CELEBRATING OUR REBIRTH

"I'm coming to the party that you're throwing for me. I read in your letter what you wrote about me. I'm coming." So writes King David in Psalm 40, according to Eugene Peterson's paraphrase translation, *The Message.*

God's throwing a party? For us? Absolutely he is. It's a homecoming party like the father throws for the prodigal in Luke 15. A rescue party like the shepherd throws for his lost sheep, again in Luke 15.

A baptismal party like the jailer at Philippi throws for himself and his household in Acts 16. A reunion party like the apostles throw for new Christians from a dozen far-flung countries on Pentecost in Acts 2.

A wedding party like the marriage supper of the Lamb in Revelation 19. A birthday party like the rejoicing of a mother over her newborn, of which Jesus tells us in John 16.

Zion Birth Certificates

That newborn? That's you and me. That's all of us, whether we came to the Lord an hour ago or as in my case, decades ago — whether we came to the cross out of Christian Science or out of some other lost condition.

Lost is lost, whether the sheep is down in a pit or up on a cliff. Whether it's eating poison weeds or cornered by a wolf. Its need is the same in every case. It needs the Good Shepherd.

We're together at this particular conference to celebrate our particular deliverance, of course — deliverance from the false teaching of Mary Baker Eddy into the true and living Word of God in Jesus Christ.

But the party isn't mostly about where we came from. It's about where we've come *to*. The home and family, the sense of belonging and of being known, that were waiting for us here all along, from before the beginning of time.

The one true church, invisible, indivisible, invincible. The communion of saints, as it says in the Apostles' Creed.[23] "One fold, and one shepherd," as Jesus says in John 10:16.

We all got new identity cards when we heard his voice and came into his fold. We all got Zion birth certificates.

"Glorious things are spoken of thee, O city of God," we read in Psalm 87:3-6. "I will make mention of Egypt, Babylon, Philistia, Tyre, Ethiopia.... And of Zion it shall be said, this and that man was born in her.... The Lord shall count, when he writes up the people, this man was born there."

This celebration is about that new birth. It's the flowing together of all peoples in God's holy mountain foretold in Isaiah 2:3.

It's the convergence of spiritual communication and fellowship among what Luke calls "devout men [and women] out of every nation under heaven" in his Pentecost story, Acts 2:5.

It's the "time of refreshing" that Peter promises will come from the presence of the Lord, Acts 3:19.

What God Did and Will Do

"Verily God has heard me. He attended to the voice of my prayer," we read in Psalm 66:19. And just before that in verse 16: "Come and hear. I will declare what he has done for my soul."

So we ask, first, what *has* God done for our souls — each of us individually, we who once dwelt in proud ignorance and put Mrs. Eddy's book of Gnosticism ahead of the Lamb's Book of Life?

We who pursued the dead-end path of self-salvation with no inkling that we were sinners in need of a savior, no inkling that Jesus of Nazareth was that very savior, crucified and risen and

[23] See full text of the Apostles' Creed in Appendix B

reigning at the right hand of the Father, interceding for us now and coming back soon.

We who denied Jesus was and is God incarnate, denied he even really died on the cross, denied we need his baptism with water, his Eucharist in bread and wine, his atoning blood as our only salvation from eternal darkness and exile.

In rescuing us from all this and calling us home, what *has* God done for our souls?

Second, we ask what does God now desire to do for others like you and me —

- some who are still trapped in Christian Science —

- some who have left Christian Science but have not yet found Jesus, who have perhaps given up on God and the Bible altogether —

- some who never heard of Christian Science but are tangled up in other false teachings, religious or secular —

- and some who perhaps have walked with Jesus all their lives and for generations past in their families, but who can benefit from the encouragement and example of the salvation story that is uniquely ours to tell?

What does God desire to do for all of those?

Third, we ask, what charge does God lay upon you and me, former Christian Scientists now enlisted as soldiers of the Cross, to do our part in his intention for saving and sanctifying all of those souls, for energizing and mobilizing and blessing them?

What is the role assigned us to play? How shall we use our time together here, so as to go home better allied to one another and better equipped in his service?

So let's consider those three questions for us all: One, what has God done for us? Two, what is he seeking to do for others, through us? And three, what is our role?

Called into Light

What God the Father, God the Son, and God the Holy Spirit did for us is beautifully expressed by St. Peter in his first letter, second chapter, ninth verse: He called us "out of darkness into his marvelous light."

Out of darkness…into his marvelous light. We can't celebrate that often enough, or gratefully enough, or humbly enough, or actively enough. We can't. Let it be in our hearts, on our minds, on our lips, in our actions, every hour of every day for the rest of our lives.

It's a fine line — to never cease remembering whence we came as onetime captives of the Mrs. Eddy cult, to rejoice always in our new freedom from that web of falsehoods and in our new adopted membership in Christ's great family — but not to dwell overly on what we were, not to define ourselves in an outgrown backward-looking way.

No, we must attend, rather, to the way King Jesus, our Savior and Lord, our elder brother and best friend, fully God and fully man, our boss the Jewish carpenter, defines us. It's Jesus who gives us our new name and our new occupation, as he gave Simon the fisherman and Saul the tentmaker.

To the ex-Christian Scientist in each of us, he says with the tough love of Matthew 7:23,

"I never knew you," healings or no healings.

But to the newborn Christian disciple in each of us, intimately known, tenderly cherished, he gives the nourishment of hidden manna and the inscription of our true selfhood on heaven's honor roll, the new name on a white stone (Revelation 2:17).

Jesus was well aware who had previously been a greedy tax collector, a fallen prostitute, a night-sneaking Pharisee, or a Samar-

itan with five husbands—but to him none of them was primarily
an "ex" anything.

Each was a special somebody in the here and now, a citizen of
the kingdom, beloved of him, beholden to him, commissioned by
him for a glorious part in his victorious plan. So are we. So are you
and I.

He called us out of darkness into his marvelous light. The
implications of that are too many to count, too wonderful to
describe, too momentous to speak above a whisper. The implications are theological, sacramental, salvational, ecclesiastical,
missional, moral, practical, personal.

But the person of Jesus Christ himself is the greatest implication of all. We escaped the darkness and burst into the light when
we came to be known by him—and know him—the Light of the
World.

What has God done for our souls? He has rescued and refash-
ioned them, encompassed and enrolled them, in Jesus Christ, King
of Kings. Just that and nothing else. But that is everything.

That All Should Repent

The next question, then, is what God now desires to do for
others, building upon what he has done for us.

"The Lord is...not willing that any should perish, but that all
should come to repentance" (II Peter 3:9).

He wants to use you and me as exemplars, evidence-bearers,
encouragers, evangelists, living witnesses.

By what we say, what we do, the way we live, and the way we
love, he wants to show people what deliverance from falsehood
and discipleship in biblical truth looks like.

We are his letter, written not with ink, but with the Spirit of
the living God, written in fleshy tables of the heart, as Paul puts it
in II Corinthians 3:3.

As the woman at the well told her neighbors in John 4:29:
"Come, see a man, who told me all things that ever I did. Is not this
the Christ?"

He is the Christ indeed. Let us proclaim him at every opportunity, even sometimes using words.

Jesus has set us apart for a special and holy purpose. It's fourfold.

One: Because of what we have lived through, we can communicate to the current Christian Scientists as no one else can, what breath-taking liberation and affirmation awaits them in a Bible they only half-understand, with a Master they half-acknowledge and have yet to really know.

Two: We can build bridges to the lapsed Christian Scientists, those whom the enemy has lulled — or traumatized — into abandoning the Bible altogether. We can help them turn homeward again, invite them back into the family of God with a recognition like never before of who God really is, what that family is.

Three: Having tried self-salvation and realized how empty it is, all the strenuous striving with no peace or security, all the spiritual pride and gnostic smugness with no human warmth, we can warn others away from that fallacy in whatever deceptive packaging it comes —

- whether political utopianism and relativistic psychobabble outside the church

- or moralistic therapeutic deism and prosperity gospel inside the church.

Spiritual counterfeits are everywhere. Our experience equips us to call them out. It's a ministry we must take up.

Four: God also desires, I believe, that in whatever denomination or congregation you and I find ourselves, fellow Christians should be aroused and stirred and heartened — and sometimes convicted — by the sparkling seriousness, buoyant joy, fierce devotion, and unflagging purpose with which we serve the brethren, the gospel, and the Lord Jesus himself.

If people at church aren't frequently saying of us, "He has, or she has, the zeal of a convert," shaking their heads and quickening their own step, we need a long hard look in the mirror. Have we gone lukewarm? Have we lost our first love so soon? God forbid.

Used in a Mighty Work

The answer to my third question, What is our role, should be evident from what I've already said.

If we take seriously God's grace and mercy in what he has done for us as onetime Eddy followers now following Jesus — if we take seriously God's intention for blessing others by the thousands, with us as his instrument — our path is inescapably clear.

It was for a sacred reason that we were taken up in the ark and carried above the waters and put back on dry land, brought here together — not merely to spare us as individuals — but to equip us and use us in a mighty work of clearing away and beginning anew.

Father, Son, and Spirit want every tongue to confess them and every knee to bow. They, the Trinity, want the falsehoods of Christian Science with all its adherents and publications and institutions and influence to diminish and ultimately disappear — replaced by gospel truth and gospel witnesses.

Toward this great goal God wants us to organize and mobilize and strategize and publicize. God wants us to self-scrutinize and be cleansed from every lingering lie or aching hurt that may remain from our days of believing the Christian Science heresy.

He Must Increase

Is there bitterness or animosity or resentment in this? No. We are men and women of the cross. We love our enemies. We forgive. We claim back from the Lord's gracious hand the years the locust has eaten.

We march with a spring in our step and laughter in our hearts. We fear nothing and hate no one. As G.K. Chesterton said about the likes of us, "They that are signed of the Cross of Christ go gaily in the dark."

Ultimately this is not about us. It's about the Bridegroom. As John the Baptist said, "He must increase, I must decrease" (John 3:30). So must we decrease as well, in order that King Jesus may be magnified more and more.

Was Christian Science an awful chapter in our lives? If it was for you, I am sorry, but God can wipe away those tears and is no doubt well along in doing so.

It wasn't an awful chapter for me, but an unfulfilling one — a time of confused wandering and worsening sin, but also of much learning, much growth.

For me it was like what St. Paul says in Galatians 3:24 about the law of Moses. Christian Science was the schoolmaster to bring me to Christ — the tutor preparing me to be justified by faith, not by metaphysical work — whereupon, as he says, one no longer needs a tutor.

"When I was a child, I thought as a child," Paul writes in I Corinthians 13:11, 12. "When I became a man, I put away childish things. Now we see through a glass darkly, then face to face. Now I know in part, then shall I know even as also I am known." That was me.

That's what the celebration is about — being known, known by the Bridegroom. "I'm coming to the party you're throwing for me," says Psalm 40:7 in Eugene Peterson's *Message* version.

Our New Song

In closing, then, let's walk through that psalm. It could have been written just for us. Psalm 40 in the King James Version goes this way:

> Verse 1: "I waited patiently for the Lord. He inclined
> unto me, and heard my cry."

As Christian Scientists we cried out to God, and he heard us. Somewhere at this very moment a Christian Scientist is crying out, and he hears that cry too.

Verse 2: "He brought me up out of a horrible pit, and
set my feet upon a rock."

We were stuck, bogged down. On Jesus the chief cornerstone, the only true rock, we found solid footing at last. Hallelujah.

Verse 3: "He put a new song in my mouth, even
praise to our God. Many shall see it, and fear, and
shall trust in the Lord."

Such are the songs we sing in true Christian worship. Such is the witness we offer, so that many may come to trust him.

Verse 6: "My ears hast thou opened. Burnt offering
and sin offering hast thou not required."

He heard us, then he made us hear him. Works righteousness, we saw, will never save us.

Verse 7 and 8: "Lo, I come. In the volume of the book
it is written of me, I delight to do thy will, O my
God."

We heard the shepherd's voice and we came. Looking into the Scriptures as if for the first time, we delighted in what we saw there.

Verse 9 and 10: "I have preached righteousness in the
great congregation. I have not refrained my lips. I
have declared thy faithfulness and thy salvation."

We tell our story now to all who will listen. We testify boldly. We no longer keep silence.

Verse 16: "Let all that seek thee rejoice and be glad in
thee. Let such as love thy salvation say continually,
the Lord be magnified."

Rejoicing and gladness, singing and celebration.
We do love your salvation, Lord. We do magnify your name.
Let our praises be a sweet fragrance to you.
Let the celebration begin!

Presented in August 2014
as a talk to the first national conference
of the Fellowship of Former Christian Scientists

ADORATION UNRESERVED

When we sing during Advent, "O come, let us adore him," whom are we talking about? None other than Jesus of Nazareth, God's Messiah.

We're not talking about an idea or a concept or a spirit-being of some kind? No, we're talking about the baby in the manger who would become the man on the cross.

There are three ways to sing those words. We can sing about adoring Jesus but not mean it, which is what Christian Scientists unfortunately do. We can mean it but not live it, which is what many Christians unfortunately do.

Or we can mean it and live it, which is what you and I would aspire to do. So that's my challenge for all of us today: Adoring Jesus for real.

Learning to really adore him will help us immensely in our spiritual growth. And it will help us in ministering to followers of Christian Science or any other spiritual counterfeit.

My starting point is from the Gospel of Mark, chapter 10, verse 21. A young man from one of the best families — devout, respectable, and wealthy — comes to Jesus asking how to obtain eternal life.

His sincerity is impressive. He addresses Jesus earnestly as "Good Master." He knows the Scriptures. He lives by the Ten

Commandments. He reminds me of myself during my forty years in Christian Science.

The Lord answers him this way: "Then Jesus beholding him loved him, and said unto him, One thing thou lackest: go thy way, sell whatsoever thou hast, and give to the poor, and thou shalt have treasure in heaven: and come, take up the cross, and follow me."

Does the young man obey? No. Does he even inquire further? No. He declines the cross and declines following the Son of God. Why? Because he can't bear to part with what Mark calls his "great possessions."

My Great Possessions

This too reminds me of myself when I was an earnest, Bible-studying, rule-keeping, possession-hoarding Christian Scientist.

Not that money or materialism or status ever kept me from considering the claims of Christ. I had all those temptations in some degree, but my "great possessions" took the form of prideful knowledge about how to know the Truth, how to counteract mortal mind, how to give treatments, how to tell the inspired passages of Scripture from all the rest, all the dross.

I was the Rich Young Ruler — not because of financial net worth or the power to boss others around, but for deeper and more dangerous spiritual reasons.

I believed I had the wherewithal, the religious assets if you will, to buy my own salvation from sin, sickness, and death.

I was confident of being able to rule myself by the sheer power of right thinking, putting off the carnal mind and accessing the divine Mind.

I knew from *Science and Health* that Jesus was not God incarnate, the second Person of the Trinity, the Lamb whose death and resurrection purchased eternal life for me, but merely "the highest human concept of the perfect man" (SH 482:19).

What need had I of him as the Lord of my life and the Savior of my soul? What need had I of his water for baptism, his body and blood in the Eucharist, his intercession for me at the right hand of the Father?

I had the highest concept and that was what counted. I had great possessions and wasn't about to part with them for any such bargain as the Cross.

I was rich — only I wasn't. How shattering and how scary, yet at the same time how freeing and how exalting, when I finally realized my spiritual poverty.

You could probably tell your own story of that tremendous experience of awakening, whether sudden or gradual — that long-resisted coming to ourselves, as the story of the Prodigal Son puts it (Luke 15:17).

He Wants Our All

The young man in Mark 10 is one of many seekers that we meet in the gospels who were interested enough in Jesus to engage with him, but not brave enough or broken enough to say yes and follow him.

There was also Nicodemus who came by night. And the man who had business commitments. The man who had to bury his father. The numerous desertions after the Lord's Bread of Life teaching in John 6.

When Jesus gave the invitation, instead of saying "yes," they tried to say "maybe" or "later" or "but." That doesn't work with Jesus. He offers all of himself, but he wants all of us in return. Exactly as he challenged the young man, we have to completely sell out for him, or we end up with none of him at all.

Oh, we can still call ourselves Christians, we can wear the various labels — not just scientific Christians as you and I used to be, but also in some cases the label of evangelical Christians or Catholic Christians or LDS Christians, or any other denomi-nation — make-believe Christ-followers full of mistaken sincerity whom we all may know right now in our own churches.

I say this not to put anybody down, but just to emphasize the fact that whoever says "but" to the Lord Jesus Christ does not truly know him—and is at risk of being told by him at the last day, "I never knew you" (Matthew 7:23).

We can't say "but" to Jesus. We either tell him "yes, yes period," or he tells us "no." We have to adore him for real. Adoration means love unreserved, love unconditional, love unending, love utterly unselfed.

It only says "yes." It never says "but." Adoration with moderation is nonsense. It's absurd. It's meaningless.

Trinity Denied

You probably remember these words from the Tenets of Christian Science: "We acknowledge and adore one supreme and infinite God." So far so good.

But listen to how it continues: "We acknowledge his Son, one Christ [and] the Holy Ghost or divine Comforter" (SH 497:5-7).

See that? Acknowledgment, but not a word of adoration for the Son or the Spirit. Nor is the man Jesus even mentioned. And thus is Trinity subtly but unmistakably denied.

During my prolonged exit from Mrs. Eddy's teachings, I struggled with years of confusion and do-it-yourself theology, trying to say "maybe" to Jesus. I clung to tantalizing phrases in *Science and Health*, like the one where she says we owe him endless homage, page 18:5, or the one where she actually says we adore him, page 26:1.

But you know what? In each of those passages, just a few words later, she undercuts it by explicitly saying, in the one case, "but," and in the other case "yet."

The unreserved adoring worship given to the newborn Jesus by the Magi at the beginning of Matthew's gospel and to the risen Jesus by the apostles at the end of the same book is nowhere to be found in Mrs. Eddy's book.

She says on page 140:10 that the only way to properly adore God is to stop struggling—her actual word is "warring"—over the mystery of his incarnation, the Word made flesh.

Well, speaking as one saved sinner, I can never be grateful enough that my struggle over that very doctrine did feel like war. It just kept on intensifying until it finally broke through my smug sense of sinless identify and my proud system of self-salvation and drove me off the membership rolls of the Mother Church and straight to the foot of the Cross.

Pricked by Truth

Much like Saul of Tarsus, perhaps like you, I was increasingly unable to "kick against the pricks" (Acts 9:5). The hints and the evidence and the clues from sacred Scripture kept battering at that good man, that paradoxically murderous man — what if Jesus really *is* the Lord of the universe, he must have kept asking himself — until at last Saul became Paul.

For me the pricks included so many things hiding in plain sight. Every Sunday in church we heard that counterpoint to the Lord's Prayer, "Adorable One" (SH 16:29). Really? How was I supposed to adore divine Principle and six other abstract synonyms?

But might the beautiful man Jesus be adorable and accessible both? That was something else again.

Up on the church wall we saw those gold letters, "God is Love." For a long time, to me, this was just one more metaphysical abstraction, stolen from the common-sense concreteness of Scripture.

Only when I traced those words back to their context in I John, chapter 4, did I see how the proof of God's love is Jesus made flesh — and how the telltale against false prophets is Jesus made flesh — and how the miraculous empowerment for selfish fallen human beings to love each other is the grace of the Father and his Son who loved us first, in all our unlovableness.

Then what rejoicing was mine. What a life of rejoicing we as former Christian Scientists can lead every day, whether in good times or in bad. Because Jesus loved us first, in all our unlovableness, transforming us into the ability to love him back, indeed to adore him, and to let that love spill on others around us — the less lovable the more they need our love.

May we resolve to make this a day of adoring Jesus for real, adoring him as never before. May we fasten our gaze on him and keep it there, as the book of Hebrews says (12:2). May we decrease so he can increase, as John the Baptist said (John 3:30). May we do whatever he tells us, as the Blessed Virgin said (John 2:5).

Such adoration is sure to bring a smile to our Lord's face — and a rich harvest in our own lives — and a new field of evangelism opportunities with Christian Scientists who so need our strong love and God's saving truth.

Presented in August 2015
as a talk to the second national conference
of the Fellowship of Former Christian Scientists

AN OLD PSALM READ ANEW

Analogy: My car, probably like yours, came with an owner's manual, including a warranty on the first page. But frustratingly, the book does not answer a lot of obvious questions. Nor does the warranty cover everything. And it expired years ago anyway.

For my life, on the other hand, for the person I am, there is a manual that does have all the answers. The God who made me and owns me has spelled out complete "user instructions" in his written Word, the Bible.

There we find countless passages guaranteeing how the Maker will stand behind what he has made — in effect, a full unlimited warranty. No exclusions carved out. No mileage limit or end date when the thing is void.

Shepherd and Sheep

May I suggest that one such warranty document is the 23rd Psalm, famously beginning, "The Lord is my shepherd, I shall not want." Most of us known it since childhood, perhaps even by heart. Its six brief verses may be almost too familiar. But when you take a fresh look at them, what depth and breadth are there.

Try reading it aloud and accenting each first-person pronoun: "I, me, my." You'll see how the warranty is uniquely personalized. You're not just a statistic or a widget off an assembly line. Jesus the Good Shepherd knows you by name. He says so in John 10:3.

As for coverage, nothing could be more comprensive. Scribbling as fast as I could to list the psalm's assurances of God watching over us at all times, I spotted over 30 of them in 30 seconds. You can probably find more yourself. Here's my list:

- Provision, protection, rest, refreshment, nourishment, healing, renewal, revival, guidance, restoration, companionship, and fellowship

- Also acceptance, affirmation, caring, anointing, blessing, celebration, joy, goodness, mercy, belonging, home, comfort, and correction

- Also support, identity, courage, life, shelter, security, warmth, abundance. And so many more.

To whom does this unlimited warranty apply? Yourself and myself, for starters, no matter who we are.

In my case as a Christian Scientist for the first forty years of my life, I knew Jesus only as a moral teacher and holy example. To me he wasn't God the Son, my Savior, the Way (John 14:6), but simply the "Way-shower" (SH 497:15). Yet even then I was under warranty from him, though scarcely aware of it.

Far Astray

No one is excluded from the Good Shepherd warranty, as a biblical word study of sheep, shepherd, and the flock will show.

But just as with a car, the warranty is of no use until activated. Insisting one is no part of the flock and in no need of rescuing, thanks anyway, stymies everything.

For me it was first necessary to see past the "God's perfect child" wishful identity pasted on me for so long by Christian Science—and then to confront my lost, sinful condition as a sheep far astray and mortally endangered. This I stubbornly resisted doing.

It took a crisis in my faith and in my marriage, recklessly self-induced, to bring about the breakthrough. The abject confession in another psalm, "So foolish was I, and ignorant; I was as a beast before thee" (Psalm 73:22), said it all for me.

I was finally broken. The shepherd's relentless dogs had cornered me at last. Surrendering still wasn't easy even then. But the reward was beyond anything I could have imagined.

That's how I came to realize that every human being is under the Maker's divine warranty. Most of us have not fully activated our warranty, however, or have let it lapse. Some have never activated it at all. We have but to ask God for the faith that leads to activation, and he will give it.

Tag, You're It

So I as a rescued sheep—sought out and saved under the astonishing "God math" of Luke 15:4, whereby 1 is greater than 99—never tire of singing my thanks for having been compelled at last to activate the Psalm 23 guarantees.

Modern-day sheepmen, I was interested to learn, clip a conspicuous pink tag to the ear of each ewe, ram, and lamb so its identity and ownership can't be doubted.

I went to a farm store and bought several dozen of them. They make a thought-provoking giveaway to like-minded friends, and I keep one on my desk as a constant reminder of "whose" I am (Acts 27:23).

Let me encourage you, then. Get into that owner's manual, Holy Scripture. Activate your Good Shepherd warranty and keep it activated. Consult it daily. Invoke it for every need.

And check the mirror often: sheep tag still there?

Presented in August 2017
as a talk to the third national conference
of the Fellowship of Former Christian Scientists

RESCUED TO BE RESCUERS

A hundred years ago in London, a drug addict named Francis Thompson escaped from the jaws of hell when he found Jesus Christ. Or to be more exact, when Jesus Christ found him.

Thompson was so overwhelmed by the experience of new life that he put the story of his rescue into a famous poem called "The Hound of Heaven."[24]

In so doing, this rescued sinner became the rescuer for thousands of other lost souls. One of those was me.

Cornered and Captured

It was 1980. I was 36 years old, married to Donna. We had met at Principia College, both third or fourth generation Christian Scientists.

We were raising our three children in the Christian Science Sunday school. I was heading up the Adventure Unlimited youth

---

[24] See poem in Appendix A

organization for Christian Scientists and serving as First Reader in the largest Christian Science church in Colorado.

But something was terribly wrong in my life. Something was missing. I began to realize it was Jesus Christ, the Son of God and Savior of the world.

Over a period of months, the Hound of Heaven chased me down, broke me down, cornered me, and captured me.

I gave my life to Him on a Tuesday in the mountains, and the next day, Wednesday, I stood before my fellow church members at the close of a testimony meeting and haltingly, rashly proclaimed Him.

Was that good judgment? No, but I could not help myself. Sometimes it's that way when the Hound of Heaven takes over your life.

Why We Gather

I love gathering with you at these conferences, because we get to hear each other's stories, join our hearts in song, and join hands to go forward together.

"Let the redeemed of the Lord say so," we are commanded in Psalm 107:2. That's why we gather, why we share.

Like the poet Francis Thompson, enslaved by opium, set free by the blood of Christ, we who have been rescued now have the opportunity to become rescuers — first for each other, communing in fellowship — and then for other "sheep without a shepherd" (Mark 6:34), Christian Scientists and otherwise, whom God may put in our path.

Escaped to Tell

Let's look at several role models from Scripture to see how Jesus the Good Shepherd intends this to work.

Start with Job, right at the midpoint of the Bible when you let it fall open. Interestingly, Job was not even a descendant of Abraham, not one of the Chosen People — but he was someone God still cared enough about to bring him through the fire and raise him up for us as a hero of the faith.

Look at the first chapter of the Book of Job and then the last chapter. Four times in Chapter 1, Satan brings a catastrophe on Job's family and his wealth. Each messenger who comes with the news says the same thing: "I alone am escaped to tell you" (1:15).

When you think about it, that's us. We made our way out of Christian Science with all its false promises and struggles and sorrows and impossible self-salvation—and now here we are to bear witness for others' benefit.

We are escaped to tell. And more than that, we are rescued to be rescuers. Skip to Chapter 42 and why do we find that God turned the captivity of Job, restored him double for all his catastrophes? Because he prayed for his friends (42:10).

They needed the light of God's truth to penetrate the darkness of their pitiful human intellect. Job at last having found that light in his own darkness, did what he could to shine it into theirs.

That's exactly the opportunity you and I have according to God's good plan and purpose, by his strength and not our own. We are escaped to tell. We are rescued to be rescuers.

Role Models

So many other examples of this beautiful pattern have come down to us in Scripture.

<u>Consider Joseph.</u> Betrayed, sold into slavery, falsely imprisoned, then elevated to sit at Pharaoh's right hand. What a rescue. But he didn't stop there. He reached back a hand and pulled his brothers, undeserving as they were, into the circle of God's grace and mercy (Genesis 50:20).

<u>Consider Moses.</u> His very name speaks of rescue from the waters (Exodus 2:10). Narrowly escaping death, he too found high favor with Pharaoh. Ungrateful Hebrews lashed out when he clumsily tried to help them. He had to flee for his life.

But God's voice from the burning bush gave him the ultimate rescue assignment: "Let my people go" (Exodus 8:1). He became the liberator of a nation. What about you and me?

Consider Peter. He screwed up so badly. We can all relate to that, right? But his Lord foretold the whole thing, commanding Simon in Luke 22:32, "When you are converted, strengthen your brethren."

Peter did, though he almost just went back to fishing. The risen Savior appeared on the seashore just in time, commanding again, "Feed my sheep" (John 21:16).

I used a little prop at our last conference, a pink sheep tag. (See previous article, "An Old Psalm Read Anew.") We're marked as members of the Good Shepherd's flock by those tags. First we wear them, then we share them. At least I believe He wants us to. No one gets a pass.

Finally, consider Paul. He helped stone Stephen to death for the crime of proclaiming Jesus as Lord (Acts 7:58). When rescued from that murderous madness, he could have stayed in Arabia as a desert mystic or gone back to Tarsus as a quiet Christ-following tentmaker.

He didn't, because he was escaped to tell—tell anyone who would listen—and himself be stoned if they wouldn't listen. Today we have him to thank for 14 of the 66 books in our precious treasury of truth, the Bible.

Heroic Women

Job, Joseph, Moses, Peter, Paul. Not to mention such heroic women of the faith as Sarah, Ruth, Esther, and Mary the mother of our Lord.

Esther was the queen. She was set. She didn't need to risk death to rescue the Jews from genocide. She did.

Mary was asked by the angel to accept an unimaginable mission of scandal, suffering, and sorrow to make possible the greatest rescue of all. She could have said no. She said yes. What about you and me?

Looking Inward

Let me be clear. We haven't gathered just to talk about looking outward and witnessing. We all need to look inward as well. We're at different stages of being made whole from the damage Christian Science can do to a person or an entire family.

We're at different stages of putting off the leftover lies and mistakes that Christian Science may have saddled us with. We're at different stages of steeping ourselves in the fullness of biblical truth, no metaphysical "key" to confuse us, no Mary Baker Eddy lenses to look through.

Our gracious triune God will be patient and tender with each of us, whatever our issues. He won't rush us or jam us into a mold that doesn't fit. He meets us right where we are. He will never, ever, turn a deaf ear to our needs and prayers.

Our Story, Our Song

The Father knows that no one ever escapes Christian Science — even half a lifetime ago as I did — without a lot of remedial work to do. And without an odd feeling of displacement that may last and last. As the Jews lamented in their Babylonian captivity, "How can we sing the Lord's song in a strange land?" (Psalm 137:4).

How indeed? Christian Science got started in the first place because a few spiritually confused Bostonians thought the Bible was no longer good enough for the strange new world of Darwin, Marx, and Freud.

Today for some of us it may be the opposite. We want the Bible, we love the Bible, but perhaps, oddly, we still kind of miss *Science and Health*. The non-Christian Science world sometimes seems like a strange land. How can we sing?

My answer is this: Newborn in Christ, we no longer let our circumstances dominate our outlook. We joyously let our outlook as adopted sons and daughters of the King dominate our circumstances.

We sing because we are the rescued ones. We have the song of the Lamb, the song of the Lion. We have the story of his Cross and the story of our salvation.

This is our story. This is our song. Praising our Savior all the day long!

Presented in August 2019
as a talk to the fourth national conference
of the Fellowship of Former Christian Scientists

Eutychus, killed in falling from a high window, is raised by St. Paul: "Trouble not yourselves, for his life is in him" (Acts 20:10).

EPILOGUE: SEVEN WINDOWS ON A LIFE

Taking leave of the reader, after so many searching questions put to others, I end by putting a few to myself. "Examine yourselves, whether ye be in the faith," commands St. Paul.[25] It's a discipline the vigilant Christian never outgrows, vital daily exercise to keep us in fighting trim as soldiers of the Cross.

[25] II Corinthians 13:5

A Self-Interview

Over the years, the Ananias website has published a number of interviews with former Christian Scientists, each covering seven broad questions about how he or she now knows God, why they left Christian Science, and what still connects them to those roots. To conclude this book, here is an interview I did with *myself*, using those same seven questions.

1. What is the faith you live by?

Jesus who made the worlds and conquered death and hell, the High King, knows me by name and companions with me constantly. The certainty of this, having him as my Savior and Lord, my elder brother and best friend, anchors the faith I live by.

God and man, law and grace, sin and righteousness, truth and duty, sacred history and eternal destiny, exactly as the Bible teaches them, define and animate my being. I find complete intellectual and spiritual satisfaction in the classical creeds: Apostles', Nicene, Athanasian.[26]

I am gratefully grounded in what those creeds call the "one holy, catholic, and apostolic church" — though still feeling myself to be a pilgrim in search of its earthly manifestation. Often I sense the faint but indelible imprint of Mrs. Eddy's teachings upon my Christian outlook, complicating but never compromising my fidelity to the gospel.

2. Why and how did you leave Christian Science?

Nearing age 40, I realized after deep questioning and study that Mrs. Eddy was not presenting the whole truth about God and

---

[26] See full text of Apostles' Creed in Appendix B

man; yet I remained a Christian Scientist for another dozen years. Religion was still a highly intellectualized affair for me.

Then when nearing 50, experience forced me to confront the ugly, elemental fact that I was a sinner, a lost soul (Romans 1:31). I sensed that Jesus was personally pursuing me — relentless, demanding, intensely loving — although it was only much later that I ever heard him called the Hound of Heaven.[27]

Holding leadership positions in my branch church and in the Adventure Unlimited youth organization intensified the ferment for me. Through acquaintances, authors, and revelatory encounters, I was being drawn into the family of faith, "the general assembly and church of the firstborn" (Hebrews 12:23), while more and more feeling myself distanced from the religion I had always known.

Both pulled out and pushed out, as it were. Hungrily devouring such writers as Lewis, Chesterton, Newman, and McDowell, I felt a rising distaste for the notion of Mrs. Eddy as equal with Jesus, of her book as a corrective to his, or of her church as truer than his.

Finally, I saw how the broken pieces fitted together: he was the Savior my sinning self had been resisting and rejecting, yet longing for. I must divide my loyalties no longer. Late in 1992 I resigned my Mother Church and branch church memberships. Early in 1993 I received Christian baptism.

It was a homecoming beyond anything I could have imagined. I wept with joy upon first receiving the Eucharist, the body and blood of our Lord.

3. What lasting effects have you experienced, for good or ill, from having followed Christian Science for much of your life?

The Quaker scholar Elton Trueblood, a writer my father loved, entitled one of his books *The Company of the Committed*. In that

27 See poem in Appendix A

broad and blessed company, Christian Scientists are one small but noble (if less than clearsighted) platoon.

So I am grateful to have joined the company of the committed for life, as a result of initially encountering the Bible by way of Christian Science in childhood — and then devoting myself to the Bible, ultimately at the expense of Christian Science, in manhood.

My formative years in Christian Science taught me to (cloudily) cherish Scripture, to trust the omnipotence and goodness of God, to rely on prayer, and to live my faith day by day. I treasure those lessons, and they are with me still.

I treasure the friendships and the role models of godliness that I gained within the close-knit circles of the Christian Science movement, especially through my long association with Principia and Adventure Unlimited.

Some habits of thought acquired as a Christian Scientist, which I am still struggling to let go of, include denying evil instead of confronting it; touches of spiritual pride and smugness; Pollyanna attitudes about health and the body; and hence, overall, an impulse toward self-salvation;.

Trueblood's real company of the committed are those who have utterly given themselves to the gospel, to Jesus Christ and him crucified (I Corinthians 2:2). Christian Science indeed set me on the path toward this full measure of commitment; yet its erroneous vestiges remain as obstacles in my path even now.

4. How much common ground do you find for dialogue between followers of the biblical Jesus and followers of Mrs. Eddy?

The earnest regard that Christian Scientists feel for the Bible provides our most important common ground. In their conviction that the God of the Bible constitutes ultimate reality and commands our utmost devotion, there is more common ground.

And yet more in their acceptance that Jesus actually lived, the gospel accounts actually happened. And more still in their thoughtful, determined resistance to materialist and secularist worldviews.

A friendly effort to explore together the implications of such congruence might ask: "Since we agree on (this or that), what do you say (such and such verse) means, or what ought we to do about (some command or warning)?"

The difficulties we'll encounter almost immediately in attempting this, however, stem from the powerful grip Christian Science has on its followers. Science is a closed and self-reinforcing belief system, defended by adherents with the dogged certainty that "It works, it heals" — for which Scientists are conveniently if unconsciously selective in the evidence they admit.

The comfortable grooves of social and family bonding among the faithful also deter dialogue; why risk disrupting one's whole world (outer as well as inner) with heterodox thoughts?

But I still welcome dialogue with our former co-religionists whenever the Spirit leads, so great is my debt of gratitude to the Christ-followers who again and again reached out to me when I was in Science. Having been rescued by Jesus, I now want to help in any way I can as he seeks to rescue others.

5. What is your approach to praying for ourselves as former Christian Scientists who are now baptized Christians?

I hope we would each pray daily to "receive the kingdom of God as a little child" (Luke 18:17, Psalm 131:2), and to fix our eyes submissively on Jesus "as the eyes of servants look unto the hand of their masters" (Psalm 123:2).

My best protection against the smugness I'm tempted to feel when comparing myself to Scientists who believe as I once did is the contrite prayer our Lord commended, "God be merciful to me a sinner" (Luke 18:13).

Then my petition continues this way: Holy Spirit, please set me free now and forever from false residual influences of that deeply ingrained Mrs. Eddy outlook. Give me opportunities to stand in the role of Ananias to Christian Scientists who have begun to ask, "Lord, what wilt thou have me to do?" (Acts 9:6).

Grant me meekness and gentleness, discernment and discretion, boldness and courage, inspiration and a winsome persuasive manner to make the most of those opportunities for your glory. Protect me, empower me, use me in your will not my own. In Christ's name, amen.

6. Thinking of someone who follows Mrs. Eddy and who may be of special concern to you or me, how might we pray for that person?

Lord Jesus, as you gently but irresistibly drew to yourself the hesitant seeker Nicodemus and the questioning woman at the well, I pray you would call this lost brother or sister home to a saving knowledge of you.

Bring the words of the Bible newly alive for them, perhaps alluringly or perhaps disturbingly, just as you know best what touches their deepest need.

Let the holy days around Christmas and Easter stir their hearts (as mine and my wife's were stirred) to see your divine beauty and feel your kingly authority despite the lulling misrepresentations of you in *Science and Health*.

Bring into their lives exactly the people they need to know and the experiences they need to have, to be awakened and convicted and converted. Chase them down, corner them, and capture them with your relentless demanding love, O great Hound of Heaven.

Use me personally as much or as little as your plan calls for, and help me remember always that this is not about me. It's about this dear one and about you, dear Jesus. Enable me, I pray, to love this precious soul just as he or she is right now — as extravagantly as you love them.

7. Mrs. Eddy in 1902 declared her belief that "Christian Science is destined to become the one and the only religion and therapeutics on this planet" (Miscellany 266:29). But obviously the path God has showed you and me for our lives went in a different direction. Another and truer religion (and therapeutics) prevails

for us and is gaining throughout the world as her system weakens. How do you see the future of Mrs. Eddy's teachings and her church in years to come?

Well, first, we can remark (with sorrow, not spite) that Mrs. Eddy's claim of speaking under divine inspiration is falsified yet again by this woefully mistaken prediction, as it is in so many other instances of her misreading of salvation history and of Scripture itself.

After another of her predictions, "that in the twentieth century… Christendom will be classified as Christian Scientists," (*Pulpit and Press* 22:9-15, dated 1895), proved untrue at the century's close, I published a sharp-edged bit of gloating entitled, "The Verdict is In."

That wasn't my finest hour—and the piece is omitted from this collection because I've realized that no purpose is served by counterposing my predictions to someone else's. What makes me so sure, after all?

Do we take to heart the admonitions of the risen Christ to his over-curious disciples, "It is not for you to know the times or the seasons, which the Father hath put in his own power" (Acts 1:7), and "What is that to thee? Follow thou me" (John 21:22)?

If so, then aren't we better off to let come of Christian Science what may come, and simply concern ourselves with following Him more faithfully?

I pray that in God's good time, the reverse of Mrs. Eddy's prophecy will finally come about, so that every lost Christian Scientist may be found again by the searching Shepherd, reborn, and "classified" among the saved.

Institutionally, the Mother Church and its branches, along with such organizations as Principia and Adventure Unlimited, may still be here a hundred years from now, ever less biblical and ever more liberal or New Age in their outlook. Christian heresies tend to be long-lived.

Yet our opportunity and obligation to witness for Christian truth are only increased by that chronic condition in a fallen world — a world does not nourish, where so many still hunger for the Bread of Life.

I therefore intend to stay in the "bread business" for as long as it takes, and my children and their children after me, Lord willing. Thanks be to God for His unspeakable gift in Christ crucified and risen, Christ reigning now and returning soon, say we all in the John and Donna Andrews family.

Published in October 2010
on the Ananias website

CONCLUSION OF THE MATTER

Christian Science told me I could think my way to health and happiness in this life, and then to heaven and holiness in the next life. This promise of self-salvation from our fallen human condition proved false. All the varieties of self-salvation, whether personal and psychological or public and political, are equally fraudulent.

"The conclusion of the whole matter," as the writer of Ecclesiastes says, summing up, is that each mortal's duty is instead to "fear God and keep his commandments…for God shall bring every work into judgment, with every secret thing" (12:13, 14).

Though Mrs. Eddy cites this Scripture, she twists it in her typical way—so that the fear of God, the judgment of God, the duty of mortals, and the sacredness of secrets were in no way ever taught me.

I had to learn them by wandering and searching, lost like Dante in a dark wood, until at last the blazing light of the Trinity, the Incarnation, and the Cross enveloped me, and true salvation in the risen Savior was mine.

I pray that these pages, in chronicling my discovery of that larger God, may help many a reader into the light as well, Ananias-fashion.

APPENDIX A:
THE HOUND OF HEAVEN
BY FRANCIS THOMPSON

One

I fled Him down the nights and down the days
I fled Him down the arches of the years
I fled Him down the labyrinthine ways
Of my own mind, and in the midst of tears
I hid from him, and under running laughter.
Up vistaed hopes I sped and shot precipitated
Adown titanic glooms of chasme d fears
From those strong feet that followed, followed after
But with unhurrying chase and unperturbe d pace,
Deliberate speed, majestic instancy,
They beat, and a Voice beat,
More instant than the feet:
All things betray thee who betrayest me.

Two

I pleaded, outlaw —wise by many a hearted casement,
curtained red, trellised with inter-twining charities,
For though I knew His love who followe d,

Yet was I sore adread, lest having Him,
I should have nought beside.
But if one little casement parted wide,
The gust of his approach would clash it to.
Fear wist not to evade as Love wist to pursue.
Across the margent of the world I fled,
And troubled the gold gateways of the stars,
Smiting for shelter on their clange d bars,
Fretted to dulcet jars and silvern chatter
The pale ports of the moon.

Three

I said to Dawn —- be sudden, to Eve —- be soon,
With thy young skiey blossoms heap me over
From this tremendous Lover.
Float thy vague veil about me lest He see.
I tempted all His servitors but to find
My own betrayal in their constancy,
In faith to Him, their fickleness to me,
Their traitorous trueness and their loyal deceit.
To all swift things for swiftness did I sue,
Clung to the whistling mane of every wind,
But whether they swept, smoothly fleet,
The long savannahs of the blue,
Or whether, thunder-driven,
They clanged His chariot thwart a heaven,
Plashy with flying lightnings round the spurn of their feet,
Fear wist not to evade as Love wist to pursue.
Still with unhurrying chase and unperturbed pace
Deliberate speed, majestic instancy,
Came on the following feet, and a Voice above their beat:
Nought shelters thee who wilt not shelter Me.

Four

I sought no more that after which I strayed

In face of Man or Maid.
But still within the little childrens' eyes
Seems something, something that replies,
They at least are for me, surely for me.
But just as their young eyes grew sudden fair,
With dawning answers there,
Their angel plucked them from me by the hair.
Come then, ye other children, Nature's
Share with me, said I, your delicate fellowship.
Let me greet you lip to lip,
Let me twine with you caresses,
Wantoning with our Lady Mother's vagrant tresses,
Banqueting with her in her wind walled palace,
Underneath her azured dai:s,
Quaffing, as your taintless way is,
From a chalice, lucent weeping out of the dayspring.

    Five

So it was done.
I in their delicate fellowship was one.
Drew the bolt of Nature's secrecies,
I knew all the swift importings on the wilful face of skies,
I knew how the clouds arise,
Spume d of the wild sea-snortings.
All that's born or dies,
Rose and drooped with,
Made them shapers of mine own moods, or wailful, or Divine.
With them joyed and was bereaven.
I was heavy with the Even,
when she lit her glimmering tapers round the day's dead sanctities.
I laughed in the morning's eyes.
I triumphed and I saddened with all weather,
Heaven and I wept together,
and its sweet tears were salt with mortal mine.
Against the red throb of its sunset heart,

I laid my own to beat
And share commingling heat.

     Six

But not by that, by that was eased my human smart.
In vain my tears were wet on Heaven's grey cheek.
For ah! we know what each other says,
these things and I; In sound I speak,
Their sound is but their stir, they speak by silences.
Nature, poor step-dame, cannot slake my drouth.
Let her, if she would owe me
Drop yon blue-bosomed veil of sky
And show me the breasts o' her tenderness.
Never did any milk of hers once bless my thirsting mouth.
Nigh and nigh draws the chase, with unperturbe d pace
Deliberate speed, majestic instancy,
And past those noise d feet, a Voice comes yet more fleet:
Lo, nought contentst thee who content'st nought Me.

     Seven

Naked, I wait thy Love's uplifted stroke. My harness, piece by piece,
thou'st hewn from me
And smitten me to my knee,
I am defenceless, utterly.
I slept methinks, and awoke.
And slowly gazing, find me stripped in sleep.
In the rash lustihead of my young powers,
I shook the pillaring hours,
and pulled my life upon me.
Grimed with smears,
I stand amidst the dust o' the mounded years —
My mangled youth lies dead beneath the heap.
My days have crackled and gone up in smoke,
Have puffed and burst like sunstarts on a stream.

Yeah, faileth now even dream the dreamer
and the lute, the lutanist.
Even the linked fantasies in whose blossomy twist,
I swung the Earth, a trinket at my wrist,
Have yielded, cords of all too weak account,
For Earth, with heavy grief so overplussed.
Ah! is thy Love indeed a weed,
albeit an Amaranthine weed,
Suffering no flowers except its own to mount?
Ah! must, Designer Infinite,
Ah! must thou char the wood 'ere thou canst limn with it ?
My freshness spent its wavering shower i' the dust.
And now my heart is as a broken fount,
Wherein tear-drippings stagnate, spilt down ever
From the dank thoughts that shiver upon the sighful branches of
my
mind.

      Eight
Such is. What is to be ?
The pulp so bitter, how shall taste the rind ?
I dimly guess what Time in mists confounds,
Yet ever and anon, a trumpet sounds
From the hid battlements of Eternity.
Those shaken mists a space unsettle,
Then round the half-glimpse d turrets, slowly wash again.
But not 'ere Him who summoneth
I first have seen, enwound
With glooming robes purpureal; Cypress crowned.
His name I know, and what his trumpet saith.
Whether Man's Heart or Life it be that yield thee harvest,
Must thy harvest fields be dunged with rotten death ?

      Nine
Now of that long pursuit,

Comes at hand the bruit.
That Voice is round me like a bursting Sea:
And is thy Earth so marred,
Shattered in shard on shard?
Lo, all things fly thee, for thou fliest me.
Strange, piteous, futile thing;
Wherefore should any set thee love apart?
Seeing none but I makes much of Naught (He said).
And human love needs human meriting —-
How hast thou merited,
Of all Man's clotted clay, the dingiest clot.
Alack! Thou knowest not
How little worthy of any love thou art.
Whom wilt thou find to love ignoble thee,
Save me, save only me?
All which I took from thee, I did'st but take,
Not for thy harms,
But just that thou might'st seek it in my arms.
All which thy childs mistake fancies as lost,
I have stored for thee at Home.
Rise, clasp my hand, and come.
Halts by me that Footfall.
Is my gloom, after all,
Shade of His hand, outstretched caressingly?
Ah, Fondest, Blindest, Weakest,
I am He whom thou seekest.
Thou dravest Love from thee who dravest Me.

APPENDIX B:
THE APOSTLES' CREED

I believe in God, the Father almighty,
    creator of heaven and earth.
I believe in Jesus Christ, his only Son, our Lord,
 who was conceived by the Holy Spirit
 and born of the virgin Mary.
 He suffered under Pontius Pilate,
 was crucified, died, and was buried;
 he descended to hell.
 The third day he rose again from the dead.
 He ascended to heaven
 and is seated at the right hand of God the Father almighty.
 From there he will come to judge the living and the dead.
I believe in the Holy Spirit,
 the holy catholic church,
 the communion of saints,
 the forgiveness of sins,
 the resurrection of the body,
 and the life everlasting. Amen

INDEX OF CITATIONS
FROM THE BIBLE
& MARY BAKER EDDY

Bible Citations

Acts 1 * 48
Acts 1:7 * 228
Acts 1:11 * 89,95
Acts 2 * 48, 197
Acts 2:5 * 198
Acts 3 * 48
Acts 3:19 * 198
Acts 4 * 48
Acts 4:12 * 150
Acts 5 * 48
Acts 6 * 48
Acts 7 * 48
Acts 7:58 * 217
Acts 8 * 7, 48
Acts 8:9-24 * 51, 52
Acts 8:26-40 * 29
Acts 9 * 48
Acts 9:1-22 * 29, 210
Acts 9:6 * 143, 226

Acts 15:1 * 115
Acts 16 * 197
Acts 16:9 * 96
Acts 16:25-34 * 29
Acts 16:31 * 30, 76, 153
Acts 19:13-16 * 51
Acts 20:10 * 220
Acts 22:28 * 188
Acts 24:10-21 * 119
Acts 24:14 * 14
Acts 27:23 * 84
Colossians 1-4 * 189
Colossians 1:13-14 * 190
Colossians 2:14,15 * 190
Colossians 3:9 * 190
I Corinthians 2:2 * 36, 71, 117, 148, 225
I Corinthians 11 * 65
I Corinthians 13:11, 12 * 204
I Corinthians 15:3 * 54, 73,147,148, 155

I Corinthians 15:14 * 110
II Corinthians 3:3 * 201
II Corinthians 3:6, 14 * 148
II Corinthians 4:16 * 1
II Corinthians 9:15 * 19
II Corinthians 11:4 * 87
II Corinthians 11:14 * 51
II Corinthians 13:5 * 221
Deuteronomy 6:4 * 120
Ecclesiastes 12:13, 14 * 231
Ephesians 4:15 * 29
Ephesians 5:27 * 59
Ephesians 6:10-18 * 51
Exodus 2:10 * 216
Exodus 8:1 * 217
Galatians 1:6 * 55, 87
Galatians 1:8 * 55
Galatians 1:10 * 55
Galatians 1:11, 12 * 46, 53, 54
Galatians 1:13-16 *118
Galatians 1:14 * 120
Galatians 1:15,16 * 47, 53
Galatians 3:24 * 204
Galatians 3:28 * 108
Galatians 4-5 * 189
Galatians 5:7 * 121
Genesis 3:15 * 50
Genesis 13:7-9 * 130
Genesis 50:20 * 216
Hebrews 4:12 * 57
Hebrews 6:4-6 * 35
Hebrews 12:1 * 103
Hebrews 12:2 * 36, 211
Hebrews 12:18-24 * 110
Hebrews 12:23 * 224
Isaiah 2:3 * 198
Isaiah 14:12-15 * 57
Isaiah 55:2 * 56
Jeremiah 2:13 * 70

Job 1:3 * 101
Job 1:6-12 * 50
Job 1:8 * 101
Job 1:15 * 216
Job 3:25 * 99
Job 19:25, 26 * 100, 103
Job 40 * 101
Job 40:19 * 100, 101
Job 41 * 101
Job 41:34 * 101
Job 42:2 * 101
Job 42:5 * 99
Job 42:6 * 99
Job 42:7 * 100
Job 42:10 * 103, 216
Job 42:12 * 101
John 1:11 * 120
John 1:29-34 * 29
John 2:5 * 211
John 2:22, 23 * 93
John 3 * 118
John 3:2 * 115
John 3:30 * 153, 204, 211
John 4:29 * 201
John 5:39 * 158
John 6 * 208
John 6:9 * 184
John 6:26 * 97
John 6:35 * 56
John 7:17 * 16, 56
John 8:31-50 * 51
John 8:32 * 127, 189
John 10:3 * 212
John 10:16 * 198
John 10:30 * 4
John 13:34 * 103
John 14:6 * 150, 157, 212
John 16 * 197
John 18:38 * 76

John 19 * 118
John 19:39 * 116
John 20:13 * 164
John 20:31 * 33
John 21:16 * 217
John 21:22 * 228
I John 3:1-3 * 185
I John 4 * 210
I John 4:1 * 191, 193
I John 4:3 * 89, 193
I John 4:4, 9, 10 * 192
I John 4:8, 18 * 191
I John 4:17 * 193
Joshua 24:15 * iv
II Kings 5:2 * 131
Lamentations 3 * 65
Leviticus 19:2 * 120
Luke 1:51, 52 * 103
Luke 1:76 * 93
Luke 1:77 * 93, 94, 96
Luke 2:10 * 70
Luke 2:11 * 103, 104
Luke 8:26-39 * 51, 52
Luke 9 * 138
Luke 9:57-62 * 76
Luke 10:17-20 * 50, 51
Luke 10:38-42 * 63
Luke 11:14-26 * 50
Luke 13:10-17 * 51
Luke 14 * 138
Luke 14:18 * 98
Luke 14:26 * 120
Luke 15 * 197
Luke 15:4 * 213
Luke 15:11-32 * 177
Luke 15:17 * 208
Luke 17:21 * 167
Luke 18:13 * 226
Luke 18:17 * 226

Luke 20 * 34
Luke 20:14 * 34
Luke 22:3-6 * 52
Luke 22:24-34 * 50, 51
Luke 22:31 * 96
Luke 22:32 * 52, 217
Mark 1:1 * 51, 69
Mark 1:23 * 51
Mark 1:24 * 50
Mark 1:25-27 * 51
Mark 3:29 * 93
Mark 4:11 * 101
Mark 4:28 * 20
Mark 6:34 * 215
Mark 9:17-29 * 51
Mark 9:24 * 171
Mark 10 * 208
Mark 10:21 * 206
Mark 12:34 * 87
Mark 16:9 * 52
Mark 16:17 * 50
Matthew 1:23 * 104
Matthew 4:1-11 * 50, 51
Matthew 5:8 * 56
Matthew 7:23 * 28, 61, 87, 164,
    200, 209
Matthew 7:24-27 * 169
Matthew 8:22 * 116
Matthew 10:8 * 50
Matthew 10:24-28 * 50
Matthew 10:28 * 49
Matthew 11:4 * 97
Matthew 13:33 * 66
Matthew 16 * 138
Matthew 16:23 * 51, 52
Matthew 18:2 * 184
Matthew 19 *138
Matthew 19:22 * 129
Matthew 19:27-30 * 138

Matthew 24:64 * 89, 95
Matthew 25:41 * 50
Matthew 26 * 65
Matthew 26:39 * 45
Matthew 26:47-54 * 51
Matthew 26:64 * 45, 95
Matthew 27:22 * 25, 32, 76, 85
Micah 6:2 * 120
I Peter 2:9 * 200
I Peter 3:18 * 37
I Peter 5:6-11 * 50
II Peter 3:9 * 19, 201
Philippians 2:1-11 * 45
Philippians 3:18 * 71
Psalms 8:4 * 1
Psalms 16:6 * 135
Psalms 23 * 212
Psalms 24 * 109
Psalms 25:14 * 57
Psalms 40 * 197, 204
Psalm 55 * 64
Psalms 66:19 * 198
Psalms 73:22 * 13, 213
Psalms 87:3-6 * 198
Psalms 107:2 * 215
Psalms 123:2 * 226
Psalms 131:2 * 226
Psalms 137:4 * 218
Revelation 1 * 138
Revelation 2:17 * 200
Revelation 3 * 138
Revelation 3:16 * 76, 115
Revelation 3:20 * 98
Revelation 10 * 85
Revelation 12 * 85, 107
Revelation 12:7-11 * 51
Revelation 19 * 197
Revelation 22 * 138
Revelation 22:17 * 71

Romans 1:31 * 224
Romans 7 * 189
Romans 7:14-25 * 92
Romans 7:25 * 190
Romans 8 * 189
Romans 8:2 * 190
Romans 8: 6, 7 * 190
Romans 8:21 * 190
Romans 10:6-9 * 110
II Samuel 12:7 * 34, 35
I Timothy 3:15 * 67
I Timothy 3:16 * 101, 102, 109

<u>Mary Baker Eddy Citations</u>

*Science and Health with Key
to the Scriptures*

SH vii:13 * 59, 106, 156
SH ix:16 * 95
SH xii:26 * 113
SH 5:31 * 149
SH 16:29 * 210
SH 18:5 * 13, 25, 209
SH 18:9 * 155
SH 23:29 * 30
SH 24:8 * 8
SH 26:1 * 25, 209
SH 39 * 118
SH 39:7 * 35, 117, 118
SH 44:28 * 156
SH 45:11 * 122
SH 46:3 * 156
SH 107 * 46, 53, 55
SH 107:5 * 5, 48, 85, 129, 168
SH 117:31 * 95
SH 123:17 * 96
SH 140:10 * 209
SH 142:15 * 70, 102, 187

SH 145:20 * 102
SH 150:6 * 94
SH 187:11 * 49
SH 196:15 * 49
SH 200 * 118
SH 200:25 * 117
SH 225:3 * 189
SH 225:21 * 190
SH 227 * 189
SH 227:10 * 189
SH 227:17 * 188
SH 227:24 * 190
SH 228 * 189
SH 228:11 * 190
SH 228:14 * 189
SH 238:9 * 67
SH 258:27 * 70
SH 259:13 * 48, 177
SH 262:17-26 * 99
SH 290:25 * 192
SH 320:31 * 100
SH 321:2 * 99
SH 361:2 * 193
SH 411:1 * 100
SH 461:26 * 49
SH 465 * 53
SH 468 * 185
SH 468:10 * 186
SH 468:15 * 167
SH 478 * 47, 53
SH 478:27 * 120
SH 482:19 * 4, 175, 207
SH 497 * 4
SH 497:3 * 31, 156
SH 497:5-7 * 209
SH 497:9 * 167
SH 497:15 * 5, 149, 212

SH 497:24 * 44
SH 533:26 * 107
SH 547:1-8 * 55
SH 547:7 * 49, 52
SH 557:20 * 70
SH 562:3 * 107
SH 563:17 * 49
SH 593:20 * 96

Other Writings of Mrs. Eddy
Christian Science Hymnal 23 * 105, 153
Christian Science Hymnal 253 * 126
Manual 17:3 * 59, 95, 169
Manual 17:5 * 132
Manual 121 * 132
Message for 1900 6 * 94
Message for 1901 34:25 * 86
Message for 1902 4:4 * 86
Message for 1902 16 * 94
Miscellaneous Writings 68:16 * 49
Miscellaneous Writings 95 * 106
Miscellaneous Writings 95 * 119
Miscellaneous Writings 191:21, 29 * 49
Miscellaneous Writings 323 * 109
Miscellany 109:12-25 * 102
Miscellany 261 * 104
Miscellany 266:29 * 95, 150, 227
Miscellany 266:32 * 88
Pulpit and Press 22:13 * 87
Pulpit and Press 22:9-15 * 228
Retrospection 30-31 * 100
Retrospection 70 * 89, 91, 94
Unity of Good 55:17 * 100

ACKNOWLEDGMENTS

I am again indebted, as with my three previous books, to the design and web-publishing wizardry of Deborah Natelson. I am grateful to Katherine Beim-Esche and the Fellowship of Former Christian Scientists for welcoming me into a faith community where many of the articles collected here took form. Publication of those articles on Ananias.org was only possible with the steadfast support of David Petteys. Pastor Kay Morrison, my Christian art expert, recommended the paintings of James Tissot, one of which became our cover.

For helping me mature in Christ over the years since my baptism in 1993, I thank a succession of faithful pastors including Scott Starbuck, Chris Taylor, Wayne Darbonne, Tom Melton, and Doug Brown. Godly men whom I have worked for and with, taught me by example more about the Christian life than they will ever know: George Roche and Hugh Fowler at Hillsdale, Jim Leininger and Fritz Steiger at Texas Public Policy, Bill Armstrong and Jeff Hunt at CCU, Ted Noble at GEM. Norton Rainey Jr., Kevin Miller, Stephen Keating, and Marshall Fritz schooled me (without their realizing it) in evangelism.

My parents, John and Marianne Andrews, while not in this life embracing Jesus as I did, taught me to follow truth wherever it might lead. And finally, heartfelt gratitude to my sainted wife

Donna and to our beloved children, Tina, Jen, and Daniel, who have walked with me every step of this unlikely path from the arid metaphysics of Boston to the wondrous cross of Calvary.

ABOUT THE AUTHOR

John Andrews has been a state senator, presidential speechwriter, college administrator, think-tank entrepreneur, newspaper columnist, TV-radio commentator, ministry executive, and naval submarine officer. Born in Michigan and raised in the Colorado mountains, he attended Principia from first grade in 1950 through college in 1966.

His family on both sides had followed Christian Science since the 1890s, and he joined The Mother Church in 1959, receiving class instruction in 1972. John and his wife Donna became baptized Christians in the 1990s, and their three grown children now also follow Jesus Christ.

They make their home in Centennial, Colorado, where John writes a daily Bible blog, edits the Ananias.org website, and serves as an elder in his Presbyterian church and as a board member for the Fellowship of Former Christian Scientists.